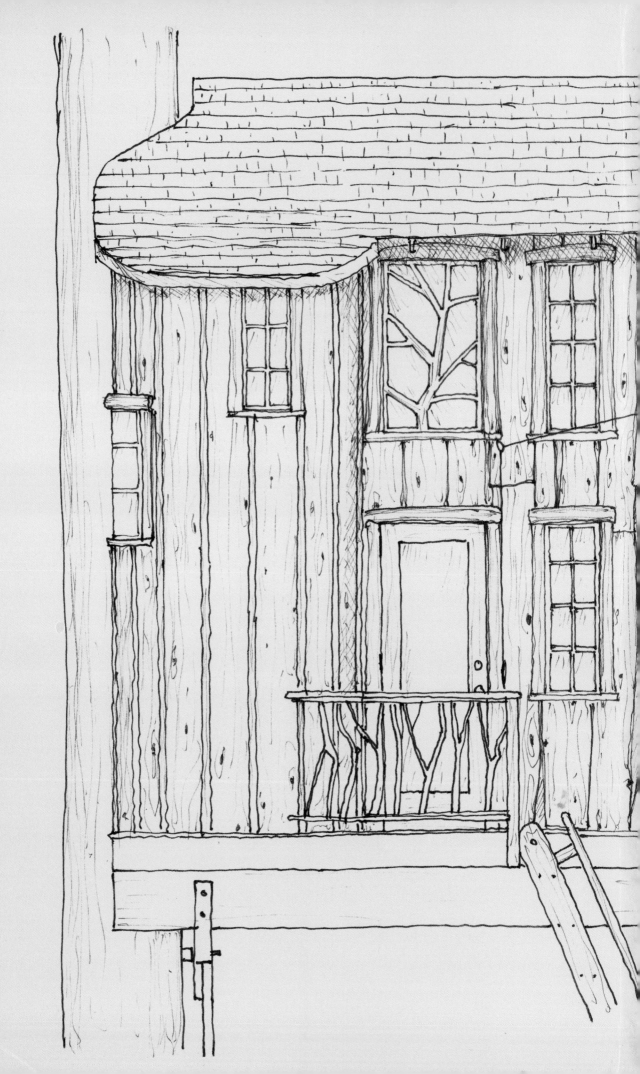

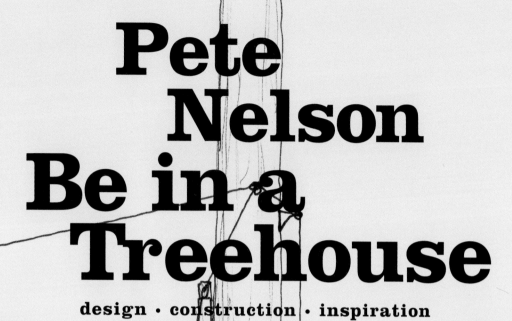

Pete Nelson
Be in a Treehouse

design · construction · inspiration

Abrams, New York

Contents

LEFT: Finca Bellavista is creating a sustainable treehouse community in Costa Rica.

OPPOSITE: The Mirrorcube, in Sweden, defies gravity and expands the concept of what is possible.

OVERLEAF LEFT: A sprawling broadleaf maple supports a more humble creation on the Olympic Peninsula in Washington State.

OVERLEAF RIGHT: The spirit of the treehouse reigns supreme in Andreas Wenning's arboreal architecture.

Introduction

It's Not the Destination, It's the Journey

I am blown away by the variety and splendor of treehouses today. The creativity and craftsmanship that people bring to building in trees fills me with joy. Never in my wildest dreams could I have fathomed the depth and breadth of this worldwide movement. It is truly glorious.

Having traveled the world in pursuit of treehouses, I have the privilege of reporting on how things look on the front lines. The United States is leading the charge, with several treehouse-only building companies and countless contractors offering the service. Europe is in the midst of a treehouse renaissance. There, the Germans are leading the way with outfits like Baumbaron, led by Johannes Schelle and one of our earliest workshop participants, Christopher Richter.

Andreas Wenning, also based in Germany, is breaking the rules with breathtaking modernist arboreal sculptures.

Farther north, the Swedes are taking things to new levels with a hotel that tests the limits of imagination. Five individual treehouses, each more unusual than the next, accommodate guests at the Treehotel in a beguiling array: One is a bird's nest, another a flying saucer. A third is a mirrored cube outfitted with an infrared shield invisible to the human eye but fully visible to birds that would otherwise be doomed to crash into it.

Ricardo Brunelli's treehouse-building company, Casa na Árvore in Brazil, is thriving—at least in the rarified air of the well-heeled. Finca Bellavista, a 600-acre treehouse community in Costa Rica, has sold out its second phase of building sites and it's going strong. Takashi Kobayashi in Japan has more work than he knows what to do with. My friend Philip van Wassenaer, who runs a specialized tree-testing company in Toronto, is pull-testing trees all over the world for people interested in building treehouse hotels.

In terms of the treehouse's safety record, so far so good—a concern as we move headlong into the fun of all of this. We must be mindful of doing things safely and correctly. Let's not hurt ourselves here. There still does not exist a meaningful treehouse association and informational clearinghouse, though we sure do talk about it a lot at the annual World Treehouse Association conferences. It is a challenge to convince building authorities that connecting to living trees is safe, but we can surely build to a standard on a level with the widely accepted International Building Code (IBC). A significant purpose of this book is to share best practices in construction methods as I know them. The last update in this regard was made in 1997 in my book *Home Tree Home*, right before the technological breakthrough of the treehouse attachment bolt (TAB). A lot has changed since then.

The book deliberately concentrates on techniques for designing and building treehouse platforms, and not on the construction that takes place above the platforms. We have much ground to cover on how to connect respectfully and responsibly to living trees. Mastering this critical aspect of building in the trees opens the door to the conventional stick-frame construction that comes afterward. Build a strong and flexible platform and you can be assured that all the effort to create the structure above will not be in vain. What you put on that platform will be left to you, but I hope the rest of the book will provide some inspiration.

First, an update on the Nelson family journey and a warm-up visit to Treehouse Point, our treehouse-based bed-and-breakfast in Issaquah, Washington, and then we will get right into it.

OPPOSITE: In Japan, Takashi Kobayashi leads a national movement back into the forest with enticing designs like this.

The Nelson family's journey has continued on a less precarious but still elevated level. Since my last treehouse book, *New Treehouses of the World*, was published in 2009, our lives have revolved around the world of building in trees. As far as the treehouse-building business was going, the spring of 2009 was a particularly troubling time economically around here. It was the end of the golden years of home equity loans, when people were spending ravenously on luxury items. When the music stopped, so did our world of building treehouses for the wealthy, or at least the moderately qualified. We barely found our chairs. In fact, it took only four months for our future bookings to run dry. People felt poor, even fabulously rich ones. And Treehouse Point, our bed-and-breakfast, almost brought our family to the edge of financial catastrophe. Let's just say that when the bank considered lending me, a carpenter, the money to buy the Treehouse Point property with a "low documentation" loan, the broker returned to suggest we modify our application and ask for a "no documentation" loan. All I had to do was sign my name. Sweet! Treehouse Point also cast us in a bad light with the local building authorities.

Oddly, perhaps, the Nelson family has fond memories of those less hectic days. Over the summer of 2009, when we would normally have been pressed to our limits with projects, we found ourselves enjoying the company of family and friends at a bend in the Raging River. "Unemployment Beach" was our name for that stretch of the river, and the rocky turn provided a setting that helped us all reflect on the most important things in life. Everyone in a small circle of friends pooled resources and came together like never before. We even got to know our own family a little better.

During this happily conflicted time, we had the opportunity to plan and build at Treehouse Point, which at that time comprised only two treehouses. The property's four acres of mature trees was practically a blank canvas that awaited our combined creativity, sweat, and toil. My mind raced with thoughts of treehouse designs and outbuildings to support them. My daughter Emily, now in her twenties, guarded the forest and reined in the overly ambitious or downright nonsensical. Charlie and Henry, our twin boys two years her junior, otherwise occupied space and were constant sources of pride and entertainment. My wife, Judy, endured the crucial and unglamorous side of paying the bills, checking in guests, and making sure the toilet paper didn't run out in the one communal bathroom.

Five years later, we are seeing the forest through the trees.

Our local building authority, the King County Department of Permitting and Environmental Review, had agreed in 2008 to allow this type of bed-and-breakfast, but the long and winding road to

ABOVE: A cairn, carefully balanced by a guest at Treehouse Point, stands peacefully on the bank of the Raging River.

OVERLEAF: The Temple of the Blue Moon, with lines lifted from the Parthenon, is Treehouse Point's most iconic structure.

building code compliance was harrowing, to say the least. Allow me to write that the old notion of asking for forgiveness rather than permission is misguided. If you are in a tough building-permit spot—and you probably are—don't go into the building of your treehouse blindly. In my experience, building authorities, once they find you, do not go away. Charm and grace will get you nowhere (not that I had any to begin with). If you choose to build a treehouse, especially one that is meant to be shared with the general public, expect to go through the same process that you would in building a regular house or commercial space. If you enter into the process with the intention of dealing with it later, be warned that you *will* be dealing with it later, and often in displeasing ways.

In fact, the Treehouse Point story has developed into a heartwarming one. While King County eventually saw the light, and they have been patient and helpful ever since, a standard planning process did not appear to be available to us at the onset, so in 2006 we naively forged ahead and built our first treehouse, the Temple of the Blue Moon, in the hopes of changing the rules. After two years of acrimony, the county shifted its position and moved mountains to guide us through a process tailored to large land development. Many years (seven, to be exact) and many thousands of dollars in fees and studies later, we emerged as a legitimate, code-compliant bed-and-breakfast with eight treehouses. A vociferous celebration ensued.

Happily, the building of treehouses for the general public has bounced back from the low of 2009–10. We have reconstituted TreeHouse Workshop, started in 1997 with Jake Jacob, into a teaching-only enterprise, and started a new company called Nelson Treehouse and Supply. The new company strives to provide all things treehouse, including planning, design, and construction, and to supply specialized materials and merchandise. We have also attracted a reality show on the Animal Planet network to follow our exploits. It's called *Treehouse Masters*. Hopefully, you have heard of it. Otherwise it maybe didn't work out.

Reality television is not really our bag, but we decided it was a good way to get a worthy message out to a wider audience. It came about one fateful afternoon in 2011, when there were only vague signs of life in the American economy, and producer Mark Grove got through our front lines and convinced us to give television a try. Treehouse orders were few and far between, but that is no excuse for signing on and doing all the things that I thought I never would—and way more. We had a blast!

The Treehouses at Treehouse Point

To give some background for a closer look at building treehouse platforms, I turn to my experience in designing the various treehouses at Treehouse Point. That experience was not entirely a happy one, and I urge any reader who is seriously thinking about building a treehouse to read my sermon on building permits (see p. 70). Asking for forgiveness rather than permission used to be my mantra. I have changed my tune since then. But once we got straight with the King County building department, we were able to create a laboratory for different treehouse configurations.

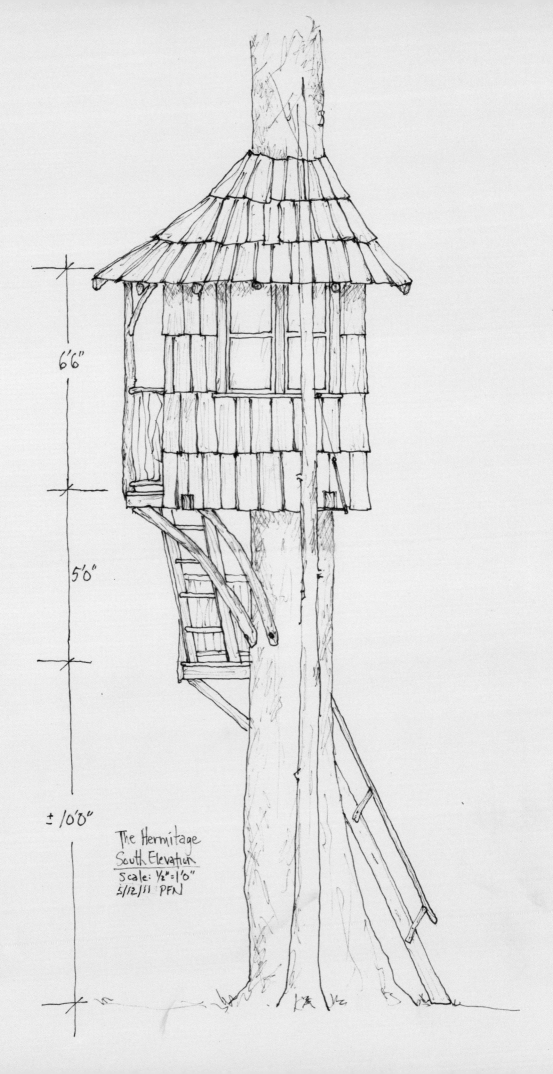

6'6"

5'0"

± 10'0"

The Hermitage
South Elevation
Scale: ½"=1'0"
5/12/11 PFN

The Hermitage

I love this tiny treehouse, which is essentially a single-tree structure with a bit of a boost from a neighboring tree, attached with paddle TABs and supported by knee braces. It could use a bed for napping, but other than that, it is perfect. The Sitka spruce host is the best part, of course, but the house's scale and size feel just right. We call it the Hermitage in reference to the simple rooms or huts that monks would use, and still do, to practice their devotions. In this case, hanging 15 feet above the clear waters of the Raging River, it feels like you are in a miniature church devoted to nature.

OPPOSITE: The Hermitage is equipped with a hinged ladder system and the rugged exterior is salvaged from the broad roof shingles of a local barn.

ABOVE: A simple desk awaits the explorer at Treehouse Point, a place we hope inspires creative thinking and thoughtful reflection.

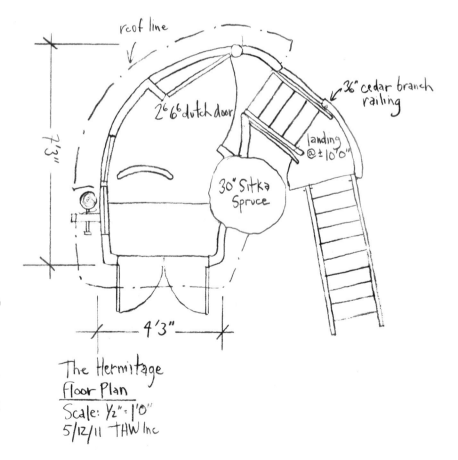

roof line

2⁶ 6⁶ dutch door

36" cedar branch railing

landing @ ±10'0"

30" Sitka Spruce

7'3"

4'3"

The Hermitage Floor Plan
Scale: ½" = 1'0"
5/12/11 THW Inc

The Temple of the Blue Moon

Charley Greenwood, treehousing's groundbreaking engineer, stopped by in the earliest days of Treehouse Point to put his stamp on the plans for our first treehouse, the Temple of the Blue Moon. It was planned as an off-center single-tree design that, in the end, took advantage of a second tree to share the load. The main tree is a mature Sitka spruce that is 39 inches in diameter at floor level. A tree like this could surely sustain the weight of the 17-by-17-foot treehouse that I had designed, but, as Charley pointed out, if there is another tree directly in the vicinity, use it.

Hence, a two-tree platform design was used. Since the spruce projects through the treehouse close to the corner of an almost square plan, knee braces are used to keep two of the farthest corners raised and level. Adding a second tree to the plan allowed room for a small outside deck—a feature no treehouse should be without.

The twin yokes supporting the main beams are made of wood and steel. This allows for easy adjustments in the field, as the angled struts can be cut with a saw to fit any situation. Most of the struts that I use today are carefully measured and fabricated off-site using steel.

ABOVE: A mature Sitka spruce carries the majority of the load of the 290-square-foot treehouse. Additionally, the 25-foot bridge is secured back to earth with heavy-duty helical screws that are more often used to anchor electrical towers.

OPPOSITE: Twin yokes are used to spread the distance between the two main support beams. This creates more room for the trees to grow and helps balance the weight of the structure above.

Trillium

The side-mount design of the Trillium treehouse came about for two main reasons: First, one side of the host western red cedar was tight to one of the main buildings at Treehouse Point; and second, the cedar is massive (46 inches in diameter at 16 feet off the ground), so the idea of side-mounting a 200-square-foot, two-story treehouse was a thrilling challenge. We accomplished it with knee braces but no posts. It offered a rare opportunity to build a structure in this way, so I present this for the purpose of showing the possibilities. It was completed in 2008 and both the tree and the treehouse are going strong.

Trillium was designed in the spirit of a timber-frame structure. The connections are all steel, however, and not the classic mortise-and-tenon type that are true to the timber framer's art.

OPPOSITE: A view of the lounge area from the sleeping loft that is accessed by a ship's ladder.

RIGHT: The soaring two-story structure sits on one side of a massive western red cedar supported by two knee braces and some high-strength cable that keeps it snug against its host.

Upper Pond

If your trees are big enough, this two-tree main support system is a great way to go. It is a classic design for a common scenario. In this case the two main support trees, both western red cedars about 24 inches in diameter at floor height, are 15 feet apart. Four TABs support two beams, which sandwich the trees. In the end, there is an area nearly 3½ feet wide on which to balance the joist level. The joist level is what carries the floor surface.

It is important to point out two features in a design like this. First, as trees move in the wind, beams must be installed in a way that allows for the trees to move independently without tearing apart the platform. Using static uplift arrestors (SUAs) in combination with dynamic uplift arrestors (DUAs), as described in the next chapter, we make one tree act as the anchor for the platform, while the other tree allows the forces of lateral motion to release.

Second, sandwiching two trees with beams in this manner often creates a narrow center of balance for a platform, necessitating additional support at its cantilevered edges. Balancing the load can be accomplished with posts to the ground, or, more appropriately perhaps, knee braces back to the trunks of the trees. This is important to the integrity of the treehouse platform and adds a critical layer to the project.

ABOVE: A classic sandwiching of two trees with support beams works well when the trees are large.

OPPOSITE: As the treehouse is accessible only by a ship ladder, guests use a pulley system to bring their luggage up to their sleeping quarters.

UPPER POND

Bonbibi

An elegant solution to the two-tree scenario that creates a wide center of balance is to use yokes. A good example of this is Bonbibi at Treehouse Point.

In the twenty-five years that I have spent working in the trees, the steel yoke system, described in the next chapter, has risen to my top choice as a practical, low-maintenance, and effective method of attaching heavy loads to living trees. It works for many reasons: It is strong, it is flexible, it will last for generations, and it makes building a platform easier and safer.

Bonbibi, named after the Bangladeshi goddess of the forest, started out as a small elevated pavilion from which to look out over the woods and river beyond; we called it the Greek Gazebo. It was the centerpiece of a spring treehouse-building workshop in 2010 and was largely completed in five days. Judy, who runs the bed-and-breakfast, suggested that it be turned into an overnight accommodation. A remodel ensued. The ship's ladder was replaced with an impeccably crafted spiral stair by the great treehouse carpenter Bubba Smith, and an all-out effort was made to make it comfortable and cozy. Today, a small deck with room for two hangs from the beams, sheltered from the elements by the house above. The upstairs feels like a stateroom in a 1930s lake-boat cruiser. There is room enough for a queen-size bed and a place to tie your shoes.

The beam layout is not perfect, as the original design was intended to accommodate a 9-by-9-foot pavilion, not the 9 by 12 feet it was stretched to become. It is a good example, nonetheless, of how a two-tree parallel yoke system works. One of its main attributes, aside from the structural advantage that a yoke allows, is how little maintenance is required once it is installed.

The yoke is a custom-fabricated steel triangle that is mounted to the tree with two TABs. The main purpose of the yoke is to separate two beams that would otherwise have to be flush to each side of the tree, creating a narrow balancing point for the structure above. Because the top cord of the triangular yoke separates the beams by 5 to 7 feet, the platform above has more support than if the beams were only separated by the width of the trees. It makes building on top of the beams easier and safer, and it can also eliminate the need for knee bracing back to the tree or posting down to the ground at the perimeter of the structure.

As in the Upper Pond treehouse, one tree acts as the anchor, and the other tree allows the forces of lateral motion to release. This

OPPOSITE: The Bonbibi is balanced on two steel yokes. The yokes spread out the load and allow for tree growth and movement in the wind. A small deck hangs from the beams below and uses the treehouse itself to shelter guests.

adequately handles tree movement in the wind, but what about tree growth? Hang on to your hammers, because the answer is surprising.

Let the trees grow and absorb the yokes! This is new thinking, but it makes the most sense. Rather than imagining that the tree will grow and push the yokes away, like a sidewalk lifted by a tree's roots, for instance, imagine instead that the tree will envelop the yoke and grow around it. It will do this readily when the yoke is bolted tight to its TABs. Meanwhile, the beams are now well away from the tree's growth area, reducing maintenance worries, narrow balance points, and knee bracing. It is a win all the way around. All you need to do is flash the ends of the beams that are exposed to weather, an important task in any scenario.

ABOVE: The inside was finished with marine spar varnish to give it the feel of the inside of a boat.

OPPOSITE: In its prior life the Bonbibi served as a gazebo. Still in evidence is the heavy-duty platform for participants in a building workshop observing the construction, installed in order to protect the forest floor from root compaction, which can be detrimental to a tree's health.

The Bird Blind

The idea with this structure was to place it at a height that no one would notice—unless they looked up. When I take people on tours of Treehouse Point I purposefully walk by the Bird Blind until you practically bump into the ship's ladder that rises off the forest floor. That's when people notice.

This 80-square-foot wildlife observatory is 21 feet off the ground in a curious combination of two marvelous trees. A 30-inch-diameter western red cedar stands up straight and tall, and a 22-inch broadleaf maple blends seamlessly at the cedar's base and stretches easterly to the river and the sunlight. It is a pair of trees that I could not resist, and in 2011 we planned and built a simple, if unusual, side-mount platform design.

OPPOSITE: Twin beam and brace supports hold the three-season structure off the unusual union of a broadleaf maple and a western red cedar.

ABOVE: The elevated bedroom has only screens to keep out the elements.

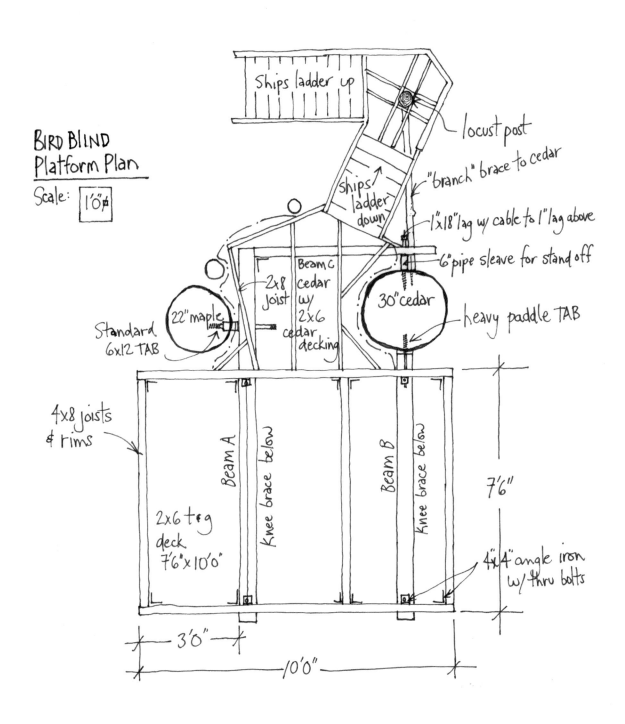

BIRD BLIND
Platform Plan

Scale: ⌐1'0"⌐

Ships ladder up

locust post

"branch" brace to cedar

Ships ladder down

1"x18"lag w/ cable to 1"lag above

6"pipe sleave for stand off

Beam C cedar w/ 2x6 cedar decking

2x8 Joist

30" cedar

heavy paddle TAB

22" maple

Standard 6x12 TAB

4x8 joists & rims

Beam A

Knee brace below

Beam B

Knee brace below

7'6"

2x6 t&g deck 7'6"x10'0"

4"x4" angle iron w/ thru bolts

3'0"

10'0"

OPPOSITE: A Seussian stairway climbs to a summertime oasis 21 feet above the forest floor.

The Burl

The biggest tree on the property is a 200-foot-tall, 5-foot-diameter Douglas fir. If we were going to build a treehouse in it, it had to be extra special. We decided to incorporate a 40-foot-long bridge for access, because the topography at that particular spot begged for one. And who doesn't love a bridge when they get the chance to build one?

Call in the engineer.

My only request to engineer Charley Greenwood was that we go with a steel substructure. We had just completed a similar steel design (John and Alex's Serious Treehouse; see p. 88), and I liked the lower profile of what would otherwise be broad and unsightly beams and bridge stringers. As I am not skilled in the steel fabrications trade, the only thing I didn't like was the bill.

Over the course of the next ten months, a revolving team of the building crew bit off parts and pieces of the enterprise. Daryl McDonald directed the steel assembly, Toby Malloy the framing, and Bubba Smith the interior finish. Devin Hanley worked on the roof and exterior finishes, and also had the dangerous job of directing and installing the stairway to heaven—a series of 10-foot-long steel ladder sections that stretch to a crow's nest 144 feet off the forest floor. That part was for the television show, and as I am not big on heights, I'm afraid Devin's next job on the Burl will be to remove it. It scares the pants off me.

Plumbing the Burl was a particular challenge. Getting water and electricity to a treehouse is in many ways the same challenge as getting water and electricity to a regular house, and depends on the climate you are building in. Building in cold climates requires forethought in keeping pipes from freezing—a surmountable problem. Getting waste and gray water away from a treehouse to a septic system is usually a matter of gravity. In the case of the Burl, however, Bubba installed a complex, albeit common, system that puts everything under pressure and pushes it across the bridge and another 100 feet to a septic system. It seems Bub has taken his already extraordinary finish skills to a new level. I wonder if he wishes this newfound trade of his to be known as a tool in his considerable toolbox. Something tells me he would rather keep this to himself.

OPPOSITE: A massive Douglas fir and sister hemlock take center stage at the Burl treehouse. One of the difficulties in designing a treehouse is not overwhelming the trees themselves—here that was very hard to do.

OVERLEAF ABOVE: Sometimes the only spaces needed are a place to sit, a place to write, and a place to lie down.

OVERLEAF BELOW: A view from the chairs out the small French doors that open to a covered deck. The writing desk is a slab of old-growth cedar that had been kicking around in my shop for years.

OVERLEAF RIGHT: By incorporating steel, the support structure has a reduced profile, creating the illusion that the treehouse is hovering in space.

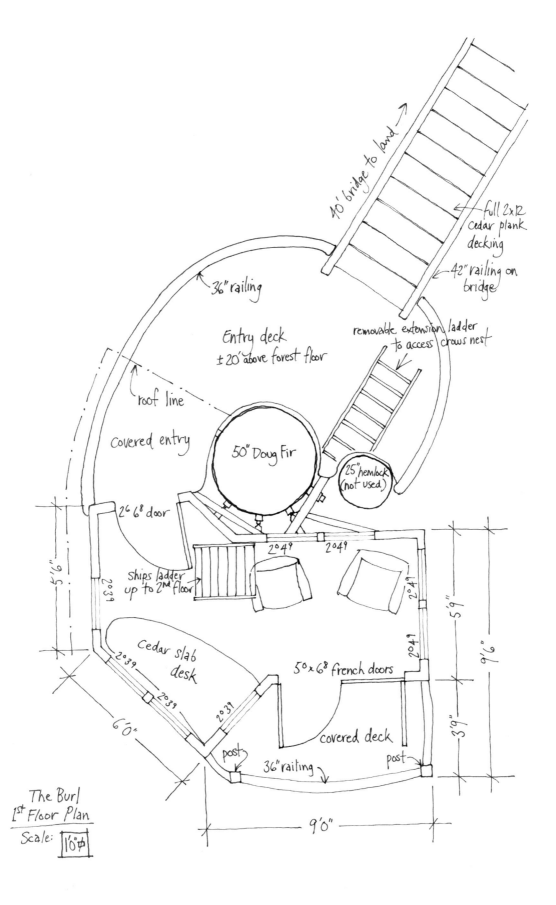

40' bridge to land

full 2x12 cedar plank decking

42" railing on bridge

36" railing

Entry deck ± 20' above forest floor

removable extension ladder to access crows nest

roof line

covered entry

50" Doug Fir

25" hemlock (not used)

2⁶ 6⁸ door

5'6"

2⁰39

ships ladder up to 2ⁿᵈ floor

2⁰49   2⁰49

2⁰49

5'9"

2⁰49

9'6"

Cedar slab desk

2⁰39

2⁰39

5⁰x 6⁸ french doors

2⁰39

6'0"

covered deck

3'9"

post

36" railing

post

The Burl
1ˢᵗ Floor Plan
Scale: 1'0"

9'0"

OPPOSITE: Three-inch-diameter schedule 80 steel pipes are used as knee braces to support more substantial steel I beams. This treehouse was built for the ages.

2

Treehouse U

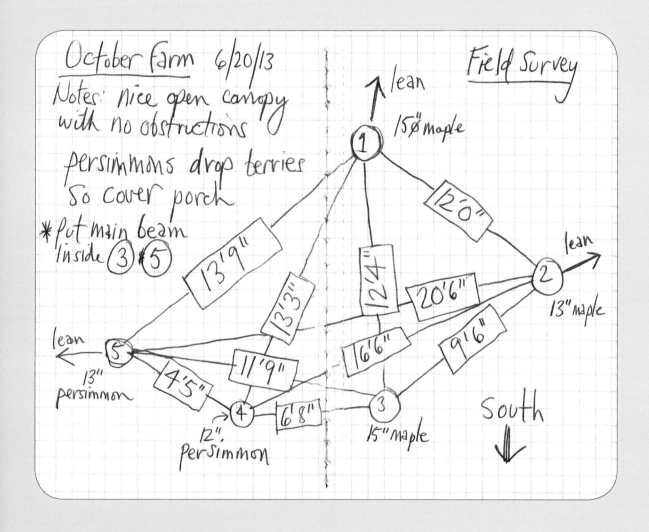

October Farm 6/20/13   Field Survey

Notes: Nice open canopy
with no obstructions

persimmons drop berries
so cover porch

* Put main beam
inside ③ & ⑤

lean

150" maple

12'0"

lean

13" maple

13'9"

13'3"

12'4"

20'6"

9'6"

lean

5

13"
persimmon

11'9"

16'6"

4'5"

6'8"

4

3

15" maple

12"
persimmon

South

I find it fascinating that people are building mostly small retreats in the trees. They are places to unplug from everyday life and gain new perspective on the beauty of life and nature. Anywhere from 80 to 200 square feet of interior space seems to do the trick. Usually they range between 10 and 15 feet off the ground and have a conventional stairway for access. Features include a desk, basic electricity, a comfortable chair, a small outdoor deck—preferably covered—and a place to lie down and check for cracks in your eyelids.

When I first started building treehouses for others I imagined that I would be building home offices in the backyards of entrepreneurs and cutting-edge office workers. That has not been the case. The occasional art studio is as close to an office as we get—if you can make that association. Writing rooms, too, I suppose. Treehouses are surely creative spaces, as they should be. The big, over-the-top, fully equipped "live aboard" treehouses are also rare, but they are gaining momentum. More often than not we are building these as guesthouses on the plots of larger "ground based" homes. The fully independent, turnkey treehouse on its own land is rarest of all. But we hope to change that.

Trees are aching for treehouses. That is what I like to believe. And why not? When one starts to really look at trees in terms of housing possibilities, excellent candidates appear everywhere. It's like turning on a light in a dark room. I tell people all the time to be careful when they begin to wander into the world of arboreal architecture. There is a strong chance that they will contract a happy ailment I call treehouse on the brain. Be warned.

Tree Selection 101

Before getting too excited about what your treehouse will look like, you need to find your tree (or trees).

Treehouses can be built in either single-tree or multi-tree layouts. The tree(s) will determine what you can build. In general, spanning multiple trees with beams is easier than trying to build a significant structure in a single tree.

Regardless of what type of treehouse you build, it's imperative that you start with strong and healthy trees. Bigger trees are usually better. Although you can safely put a TAB in a healthy tree as small as 10 inches in diameter, larger trees are ideal because they tend to move less in the lower reaches than smaller trees and have been put through their paces in terms of pest and fungus attacks and spells of drought. If you are planning a treehouse in a single tree, make sure the tree is at least 18 inches in diameter. If your treehouse uses multiple trees, try to select ones that are within 16 to 18 feet of each

PREVIOUS PAGE, FIGURE 1: An example of a typical field survey delineating the distances between trees in all of their possible combinations.

other. Naturally, larger spans require larger beams, and larger beams quickly become significantly more cumbersome to work with.

While treehouses can be built at almost any height, there are a few factors to consider that may make your project safer and more enjoyable to build. It is important to keep in mind that the higher up you go, the more the tree will move and the more difficult your treehouse will be to build. I recommend building within safe reach of a good ladder, so you can easily get yourself, your structure, and your materials in place. We are also big proponents of building scaffolding to ensure a safe and comfortable working environment in the air. A good rule of thumb is to aim for a height between 10 and 20 feet from the ground.

When choosing where to build, the site can be as important as the trees themselves. Ask yourself questions like "How will I get lumber and tools to the site?" "Will I get the view that I am looking for?" "How much sunlight does this site get?" "How will this treehouse affect my neighbors?" "How can I get power to the site?" and so on. I love the architecture adage that suggests you should resist the urge to build on the most beautiful part of the site, so as to preserve its beauty for your view. A complete understanding of the environment in which you plan to build will help ensure a successful project.

Once you think you know which trees you want to use for your treehouse, consider getting an arborist to verify the health of the trees. Arborists are very knowledgeable about how healthy and structurally sound the trees might be. Every tree is different, and some trees are more ideally suited for supporting treehouses than others, so please get your trees evaluated to ensure that they have no structural problems and can continue to support a treehouse for a long time.

I'd like to think that any tree is a good tree for building in, but the following lists offer a good starting point for selecting the best ones.

Ideal Trees

Apple, ash (be careful of blight in the midwestern United States), beech, cedar, chestnut, cypress, Douglas fir, elm, larch, London plane, all maples, monkeypod, almost all oaks, redwood, spruce, and sycamore

Acceptable Trees

Avocado, basswood, bay, birch, catalpa, cherry, eucalyptus, gingko, hackberry, hemlock, hickory, hornbeam, ironwood, lime, locust, madrone, magnolia, mulberry, olive, Osage orange, persimmon, pine (watch for the beetle kill blight in the northern and western United States), poplar, sassafras, sweet gum, walnut, willow, and yew

Bad Trees (Okay, I guess there are a few . . .)

Alder, aspen, box elder, cottonwood, holly, juniper, palm, and swamp oak

The Tree Layout Plan

In order to begin to design a treehouse, you will need to make a drawing showing all of the tree trunks and major branches in the location of your treehouse, whether or not you will ultimately use them for support. We call this drawing a tree layout plan. This crucial drawing shows the diameters of the tree trunks and branches, and also the distances between them.

For a useful tree layout plan, you'll need to take accurate measurements. The trees often do not sit on perfectly level ground, so be sure that your measurements are level in relation to each other and not with the ground. For complex tree layouts, you may want to use a string level or a water level to make sure your measurements are at the same height. For simpler tree layouts you should only need your eye.

A simple way to begin is to make a rough sketch of the trees you plan to use before you begin the measurement process. Don't worry about scale at this point—that will come in later. You can work in a notebook, first drawing and numbering the trees, and drawing a box for each measurement that you can fill in as you go (Fig. 1). Next, using lines centered on each tree, measure the distances "from bark to bark" between them, as well as the diameters of all the trees, and write them down in the sketch. If you are by yourself, bring string to tie around the trunks so you can hook the end of your tape measure to it when pulling measurements between trees. Also, you may want to mark the trees with surveyor's tape so you don't forget which ones you picked.

You should also record important details, like which direction south is (look for the sun and try to make a guess). Draw arrows indicating any leans to the trees if they are significant, and note any branch obstructions within the tree canopy that you might wish to keep; trees can handle a solid pruning if blocking branches need "modification."

Using the sketch, you can create a scaled tree layout plan that accurately shows the tree sizes and the distances between the trunks and branches (Fig. 2). I recommend making this drawing on graph

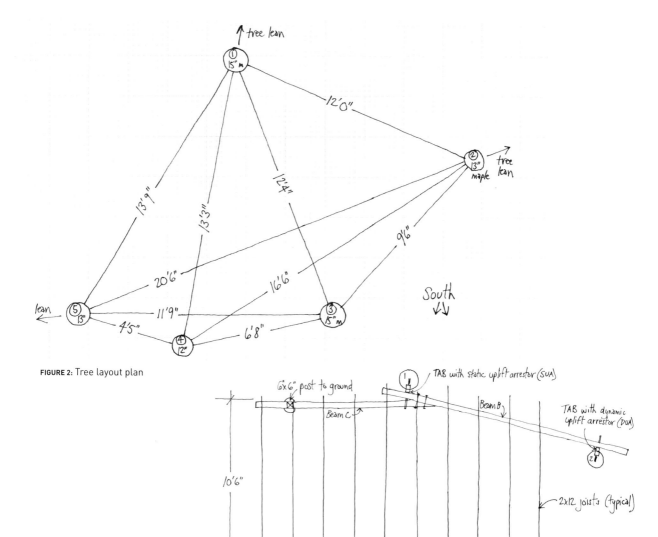

FIGURE 2: Tree layout plan

FIGURE 3: The beginnings of something

paper, for simplicity and clarity. A carefully created tree layout plan is essential for designing a treehouse from scratch (Fig. 3).

Now, before we start really getting into the nitty-gritty of planning a platform, we need to cover basic treehouse design logic and introduce the hardware you'll use to build it.

Treehouse Design Logic

Standing in a calm, quiet forest sometimes feels like being in a tremendous natural cathedral. The trees stand tall and straight, holding up the vaulted sky above. When the wind blows, there is a realization that the trees are not columns, but great big creatures that move on their own, swaying to their own rhythms. Trees are alive and dynamic. They are the foundations of treehouses, but they cannot be thought of as still, static columns. They must be allowed

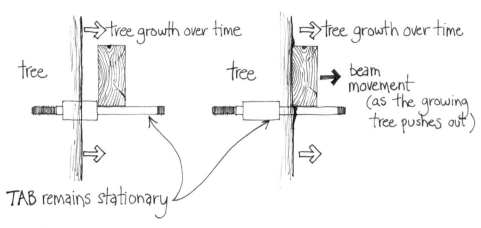

FIGURE 4: Tree growth

their movement. Trying to prevent this natural motion is harmful to the tree's health and catastrophic for a treehouse's structural integrity. Thus, the two dynamic forces that govern treehouse platform construction are *tree growth* and *tree movement*. We must design around these forces, focusing on providing sound structural support no matter which way the trees decide to move or grow. It is a challenge, but with careful planning and the right hardware, a treehouse can embrace the trees' natural growth and rhythm, resting safely among them for decades to come.

Allowing for Tree Growth

Trees grow in two different directions: upward and outward. Upward tree growth only happens at the tops and tips of the trees. This means that your treehouse will stay at a constant height from the ground even as the trees grow taller. Increasing tree girth is the only growth factor we consider in design.

The TABs (treehouse attachment bolts) that you will use to anchor your platform are designed to allow for increases in tree girth. As the tree grows, it will envelop more and more of the TAB, eventually pushing the beam outward along the shaft, rather than pushing the entire piece of hardware out of the tree (Fig. 4). It should be noted, however, that sometimes trees will choose to envelop a beam rather than force the issue.

Over time, as the beams move because of tree growth, their positions with respect to other beams also changes. Therefore, just as beams cannot be rigidly connected to trees, the joists that sit on the beams and support the platform deck cannot be rigidly connected to all beams. Instead, when building a treehouse, it is necessary to attach joists to only one beam. The other end of the joists will simply sit on top of the other beams, allowing for a free range of motion. With proper blocking between joists and decking over the joists, you create a strong diaphragm that floats over the beams where the joists are not rigidly attached.

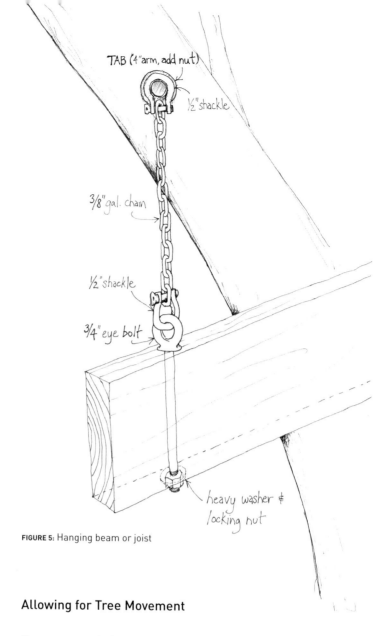

TAB (4"arm, add nut)

½" shackle

3/8" gal. chain

½" shackle

3/4" eye bolt

heavy washer & locking nut

FIGURE 5: Hanging beam or joist

Allowing for Tree Movement

Trees sway at their own rates, to their own rhythms, regardless of how other trees are moving around them. When building a treehouse that involves more than one tree, it is important to allow for independent tree movement, rather than rigidly fixing trees together with beams or other structural components. You'll use a piece of hardware called the dynamic uplift arrestor to safely connect a beam to more than one tree while still allowing for lateral tree movement.

The height at which the treehouse is built will also factor in to how much tree movement to account for. The higher in the tree you build, the more the tree will move in the wind, which is why we strongly suggest that you build your treehouse in the lower quarter of the tree. The maximum movement allowed by a large dynamic uplift arrestor is 14 inches, which is usually plenty of range. However, if your treehouse is especially vulnerable to wind, you can still make a treehouse work. TABs are great for hanging loads, too. If your tree movement is too great for a dynamic uplift arrestor, you may be able to use cable or chain to hang a load, thereby giving it maximum flexibility of movement (Fig. 5).

OPPOSITE ABOVE: This TAB was installed in the year 2000. The oak tree quickly grew and sealed around the 3-inch diameter "boss." The picture also shows an imprint of the nut that attached to the end of the TAB, which we had to extend.

OPPOSITE BELOW: This is an example of how a tree "bolster blocks" around a beam, If the tree cannot move the beam, it will grow around it.

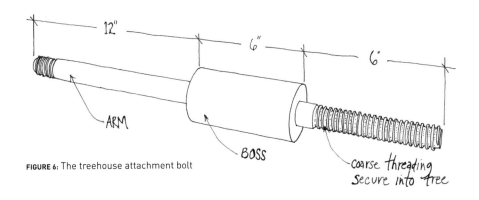

FIGURE 6: The treehouse attachment bolt

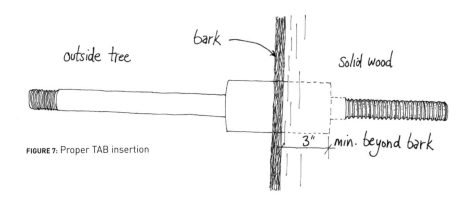

FIGURE 7: Proper TAB insertion

Treehouse Hardware 101

The Treehouse Attachment Bolt—aka the TAB

The TAB—the treehouse attachment bolt—is the most important piece of technology in treehouses today.

This groundbreaking—bark-breaking—device has a tangled history that began at the first annual World Treehouse Conference in Takilma, Oregon, in 1997. Suffice to say that the technology behind it is in the public domain and that no one holds—or ever can hold—a patent on its basic parts.

The very best way to successfully mount a treehouse in a living tree is with a simple and extremely strong steel bolt. Without the TAB, we could not safely accomplish so many things with our treehouses. A sturdy chunk of hardened steel, this heavy piece of hardware acts like an artificial tree limb. The main structural support members for the treehouse will rest on or hang from the TABs. A standard-size TAB can support between 6,000 and 10,000 pounds of force, depending on what type of tree is being used. Softer trees, such as pines and cedars, will support closer to 6,000 pounds, while harder trees, such as oaks and maples, will support closer to 10,000 pounds, but there are many other factors contributing to the TAB's ultimate holding power.

The TAB is made from two separate pieces of steel (Fig. 6). The first is a length of 1¼-inch-diameter round stock 4140 steel, and the

This is a standard 6-by-12-inch TAB installed properly. Note that the 6-inch boss is halfway into the wood of the tree.

second is a length of 3-inch-diameter round stock mild steel that is press-fitted onto the narrower piece. Each TAB is custom fabricated in a machine shop and, when complete, is composed of four main sections, which can be seen in Fig. 6. The coarsely threaded end will secure the TAB within the heartwood of a tree. The *boss*, the thicker piece of 3-inch-diameter steel, provides the majority of the TAB's sheer strength and allows for greater distribution of the load. The *arm* extends outward from the boss and acts as a limb to support the beams or other structural members. At the end of the arm is a short threaded section designed to accommodate the K-nut, which will be discussed later.

When properly installed, the coarsely threaded end and half of the boss penetrate the tree (Fig. 7). It is important to note that half of the boss will go beyond the bark and into the solid, healthy wood. Bark is not strong and has no structural value. The standard TAB is designated as 6 by 12 inches. This measurement refers first to the length of the boss (6 inches is standard), and then to the length of arm—the end sticking out of the tree (12 inches is standard). There are variations in both of these lengths and in the diameters of bosses and arms themselves, depending on the use.

The TAB works effectively because it not only supports large loads, but also allows free growth of the tree. The tree reacts to a TAB by growing what is called *reaction wood* around the perimeter of the boss. This seals off any possibility of airborne fungus and disease infiltrating the tree. Nutrients continue to flow both up and down the important cambium layer of the tree, just below the bark, and the tree continues to grow in its normal fashion. As the tree envelops it, the TAB becomes stronger. Cutting off the flow of nutrients by girdling or somehow belting a tree will eventually kill it. An adjustable belt, which I have seen employed on occasion, is ill-advised, in my opinion. I worry that the adjustment will not happen as the tree grows greater in girth, and the tree will suffer and die.

Uplift Arrestors

The beams that support the treehouse platform normally rest on the arm of the TAB. The uplift arrestor is a piece of hardware attached to the bottom of a beam, preventing the beam from lifting up or pulling away from the TAB, while still allowing the beam to move laterally along the length of the TAB's arm over time. TABs and uplift arrestors work together to provide a strong and dynamic support system that allows for tree growth and movement without sacrificing the integrity of the structure or harming the trees. We have created two types of uplift arrestors that serve slightly different purposes: the dynamic uplift arrestor and the static uplift arrestor.

The dynamic uplift arrestor (Fig. 8) allows lateral movement along the length of the TAB's arm while preventing vertical movement of the beam, and its slot design also allows tree movement perpendicular to the TAB (Fig. 10). In other words, if a tree supporting a beam begins to sway in the wind, the beam will remain relatively stationary, as the TAB simply moves back and forth within the slot of the dynamic uplift arrestor. The beam can easily slide over the TAB thanks to a piece of UHMW (ultrahigh-molecular-weight polyethylene, a high-density, low-friction material) secured within the slot. This allows smooth and fluid movement of the TAB arm within the arrestor.

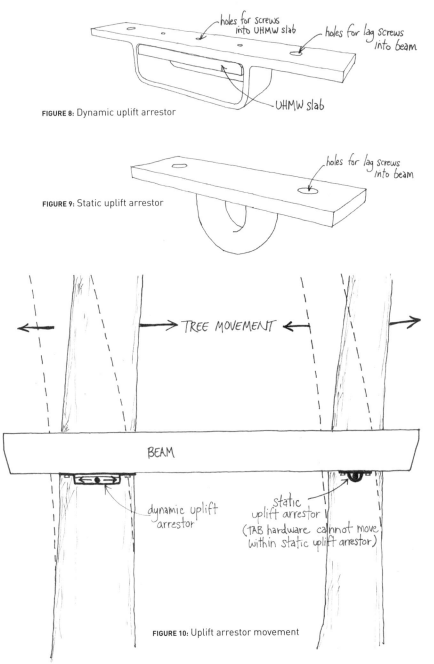

FIGURE 8: Dynamic uplift arrestor

FIGURE 9: Static uplift arrestor

FIGURE 10: Uplift arrestor movement

The static uplift arrestor (Fig. 9) is also used to secure a beam to a TAB, although it restricts any movement of the beam perpendicular to the TAB (Fig. 10). These static arrestors are commonly used in single-tree structures. They can also be used at one end of a beam spanning two trees, where the other end is secured with a dynamic uplift arrestor—Upper Pond Treehouse platform (p.24) is an example of this arrangement, which protects the platform from the lateral forces of tree movement.

K-Nut and Suspender Unit—aka the Dynamic Triangle

As a tree grows, it may choose to push your beams outward along the arm of the TAB. We add extra strength and structural life span to the TAB by supporting the end of it with a cable suspension assembly called the *dynamic triangle*. To support the exposed end, a K-nut is threaded onto the end of the TAB after the beams have been properly installed using uplift arrestors. A turnbuckle is then connected to the K-nut and a 2- to 4-foot-long cable sling is fastened to the other end of the turnbuckle. The unconnected end of the cable sling is fastened to the tree with a 1-by-8-inch lag bolt. The turnbuckle is tightened by hand to remove the slack, and the dynamic triangle is complete (Fig. 11). This whole assembly works together as one unit to ensure that

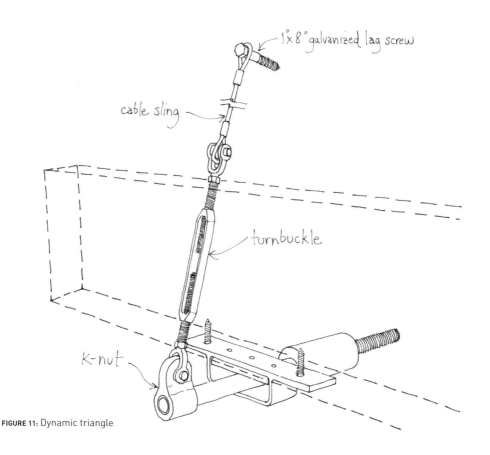

FIGURE 11: Dynamic triangle

the beam's perch has maximum structural integrity for as long as possible; it is part of a standard connection system.

There are occasions when going below the TAB for additional support, rather than above it, works more effectively—we call this the *reverse dynamic triangle*. When dealing with heavy loads, we like to use an adaptation of a top-link connector, which is a device that farmers use to keep their tractor plows driving down into the earth. It works like a turnbuckle, only it separates loads rather than pulling them together.

Knee Brace

In the treehouse business, we spend a lot of time trying to maximize platform size in limited-tree configurations. In many cases, you will find that you need some extra structural support at the end of a beam, or some platform space where you do not have a beam to rest it on. In these cases, we can use a wooden knee brace that extends down at an angle from the edge of a platform to the lower part of a tree to accomplish what we need (Fig. 12). The geometry and pressure of the connection provide the strength necessary to hold the weight of a beam or floor away from the trunk of a support tree without posting down to the ground. With the correct hardware and careful installation, this can be an excellent way to increase the size of a treehouse platform when you are limited by a lack of other trees to tie to. Sure, a post to the ground can accomplish the same thing, and there are plenty of situations where a post, or *ground-mounted strut*, as our engineer, Charley Greenwood, likes to call it, is in order. But from a purist's point of view, a knee brace is neater.

ABOVE LEFT: A reverse dynamic triangle. The vertical member is a common top link found in tractor supply stores that keeps heavy loads separated.

ABOVE RIGHT: Two knee braces support the cantilevered edge of the Upper Pond treehouse at Treehouse Point.

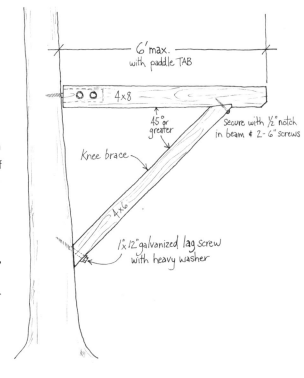

FIGURE 12: The paddle TAB and knee brace

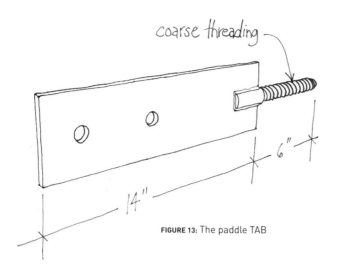

coarse threading

FIGURE 13: The paddle TAB

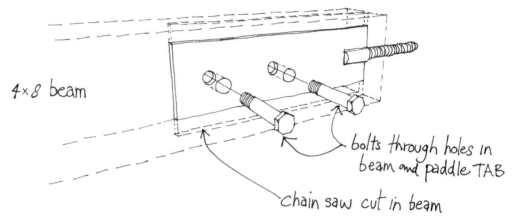

4 × 8 beam

bolts through holes in beam and paddle TAB

chain saw cut in beam

FIGURE 14: The paddle TAB in beam

The Paddle TAB

The paddle TAB is designed for the installation of smaller treehouse structures and components. It consists of two sections: the *paddle*, a flange that supports a structural element, and welded to it, a threaded rod that is screwed into the tree (Fig. 13). A major difference between this design and the standard TAB is the lack of a boss, which is the piece of the standard TAB capable of resisting large sheer forces. By not having a boss, the paddle TAB is easier to install in a tree, but it also holds significantly less weight. Once the paddle TAB is secured in the tree, a notched beam can be fitted onto the paddle section and bolted in place (Fig. 14). This hardware is used almost exclusively in conjunction with a knee brace assembly (Fig. 12)—an example is the Hermitage platform design (p. 19). By using multiple paddle TABs and knee braces around a tree (typically, five), an efficient platform can be constructed. As a rule of thumb, however, paddle TABs should not be used with beams that are longer than 6 feet, or ones that are bearing unusually large loads—like a hot tub, for instance.

The Yoke

The yoke is not, strictly speaking, a piece of hardware. It is usually prefabricated in wood, steel, or a combination of the two and used as a substructure to support beams. Yokes are often used in two- and three-tree treehouses when beams resting on TABs would not provide a wide enough structural base. Regardless of its composition, a yoke is an angle of 45 degrees or greater that is connected to a tree with two vertically mounted TABs (Fig. 15).

The two yokes supporting each end of their two beams are bolted statically to their trees, but they can be easily incorporated into a dynamic structural plan: The anchor tree yoke holds both beams statically, bolted through the upright steel flanges at both ends of the yoke. The other yoke allows both beams to slide, guided by twin upright steel flanges (unbolted) and plastic skid plates, as the trees move. The platform plan for the Bonbibi treehouse at Treehouse Point (p. 27) uses this arrangement.

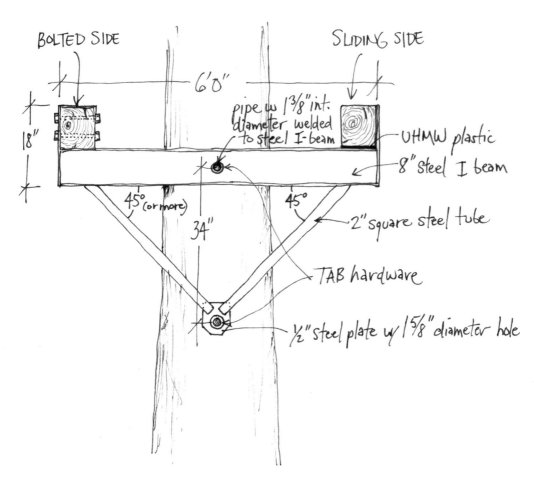

BOLTED SIDE   SLIDING SIDE

6'0"

18"

pipe w/ 1⅜" int. diameter welded to steel I-beam

UHMW plastic

8" steel I beam

45° (or more)   45°

2" square steel tube

34"

TAB hardware

½" steel plate w/ 1⅝" diameter hole

FIGURE 15: Steel yoke showing both bolted and sliding sides

OPPOSITE: It is imperative that the TABs be installed precisely so the prefabricated steel yoke fits over them.

RIGHT: This yoke has a 7-foot-wide spread and is installed 18 feet off the forest floor.

Platform Design 101

Now that you understand the principles of treehouse design logic and have become familiar with treehouse hardware, you can start putting pencil to paper to design your treehouse platform. Allow the trees to guide the process. Look to the trees and listen to your own design intuition.

It's time to start getting excited about how the treehouse will look. This is one of my favorite parts in creating a treehouse, and I strongly urge anyone embarking on this path to take the time to enjoy and plan carefully. A successful project is born of a good plan, and a good plan is based on a sound platform. Every treehouse consists of two major elements: the *platform* and the *shell*. The platform is the structural foundation, and it consists of all the structural components— hardware, beams, joists, and decking surface—that will eventually

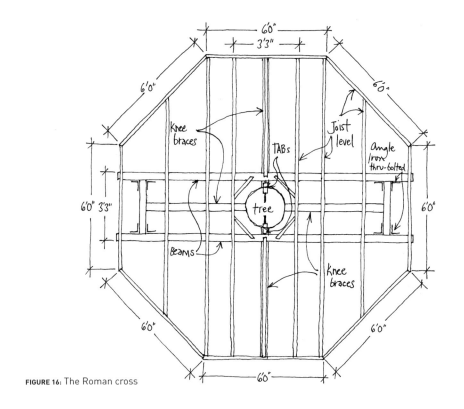

FIGURE 16: The Roman cross

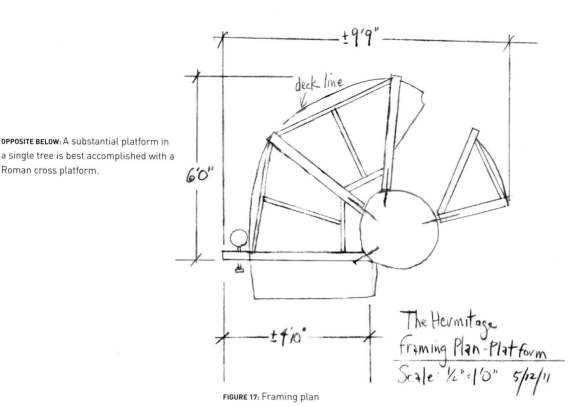

OPPOSITE BELOW: A substantial platform in a single tree is best accomplished with a Roman cross platform.

± 9'9"

deck line

6'0"

± 4'0"

The Hermitage
Framing Plan - Platform
Scale: ½" = 1'0"   5/12/11

FIGURE 17: Framing plan

support the shell. Just as the foundation is the most important part of your house, the platform is the most important part of your treehouse. The shell is everything above the decking: walls, windows, doors, and roof. Designing the platform must happen first, since this is what determines the size and shape of everything to follow.

If you plan on building a single-tree treehouse, there are only two types of platforms I recommend: the Roman cross (Fig. 16), where two main beams sandwich a single tree and a floor joist layer sits on top of the beams, for larger platforms with a radius 6 to 8 feet off the bark of the tree and no more, and paddle TAB platforms (Fig. 17) for smaller platforms 6 feet or less off the bark of the tree.

When spanning multiple trees, there are endless beam-and-joist combinations that can be used to create the platform on which your treehouse will sit. Using the accurately scaled tree layout diagram created earlier, you can begin playing with configurations of beams spanning the trees. See Fig. 18 for a few different examples of how beams can be positioned for different tree layouts.

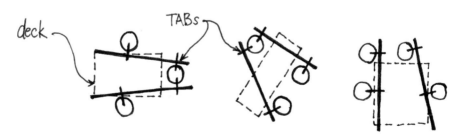

deck   TABs

FIGURE 18: Beam layout examples

PLATFORM DESIGN 101   57

Designing a platform starts with placing the beams, and the sizes of the beams will depend on the distance they will have to span and the weight they will have to carry. The beams will support the joists, and the joists must be strong enough to span the distance between the beams and support the treehouse. Our standard deck is made with 2-by-12-inch nominally cut Douglas fir or yellow pine joists sitting on top of large fir beams or engineered glue-laminated wooden beams (which can range anywhere from 3½ by 12 inches to 6 by 19 inches, or even larger), but I suggest that you consult the published sawn lumber and engineered wood span tables (available on several trustworthy websites, including the American Wood Council's at www.awc.org) to determine a safe size for your structural members. You can also have your structure checked by a licensed structural engineer, although he or she will probably freak out about connecting to a living tree! Maybe just tell him to imagine there is a post there instead of a tree . . . and then assure him that his name will never come up again in association with your harebrained scheme.

After planning the placements of the beams, joists, and platform deck, you can move on to your treehouse shell. I always start the outline or floor plan of a design by drawing possible walls 9 inches off the bark of all trees. This gets the process moving and keeps things from getting bogged down or overwhelming. With a little imagination, it can take almost any form. Have fun—the possibilities are endless. For important and helpful tips on some specific design elements, consult the rules of thumb below.

Rules of Thumb

While all building projects present specific challenges, here are a few guidelines to keep in mind when planning and building your treehouse.

Approximate clearances for platform and enclosure

- Keep 3 inches (or more, if possible) between the beams and the bark of a tree.
- Keep joists 6 to 9 inches away from the bark of a tree (depending on how soon you want to get out the reciprocating saw and do a "remodel").
- Keep walls and roofs 9 inches away from the tree, if possible.
- Trim decking 1½ inches back from the bark of the tree, then be ready to trim it back with a jigsaw every six or eight years, depending on how quickly your tree grows.

OPPOSITE : Patrick Willse is on the adjustable end of a water level, one of the most important tools of a treehouse builder. A water level is an extremely accurate way of finding level in relation to a single point between two trees. Plus it can even see around the backs of trees when needed!

- Keep trunks and branches from penetrating the envelope of the building if you want to control the environment inside your treehouse.

Platform Construction Basics

With the design complete, it is time to head up into the trees and start building your dream treehouse. The first step will be installing the hardware that will support the beams. Using the specialized hardware described in this book requires thorough preparation and careful installation. If the hardware is installed incorrectly, it cannot be corrected easily. The most important thing to do is to sink the boss of the TAB the full desired depth into the wood of the tree. The bark of the tree has zero structural value and therefore does not count for anything.

Step 1: Measuring TAB Locations

To begin, we need to mark exactly where our TABs go. When creating a tree layout plan, the trees are measured at the approximate height where the treehouse structure will sit, but this is not where the TABs will go. The TAB is typically installed below the floor level at a distance equal to the depth of the decking, joists, and main beam combined. Now that it is time for installation, we need to be more precise. In order to ensure that our structure sits level across our trees, we recommend that you employ a tool called a water level (Fig. 19). This is old technology, as old as Egypt, but it is the best method to guarantee the beams will lie level over the TABs. The water

FIGURE 19: Using a water level

level is a useful tool because it can show level when you are far away from your first point, or when your line of sight is interrupted by a tree. The water levels sold as kits have an electronic sensor to allow you to take measurements on your own, but if you have any helpers on your project, just fill the clear plastic tube with water—making sure to get rid of any air bubbles—and you can get started.

The following example will demonstrate how to easily mark the locations where the TABs will be installed in the trees. For this example we will pretend we are placing a beam between a cedar tree and a maple tree 12 feet apart from each other on uneven ground.

Step 2: Leveling

A screw is placed in the maple 7 feet above the ground—the height where the TAB is expected to be installed. Try to insert your screws at approximately the same spot on the tree where you will be drilling. Using the first screw as a point of reference, use the water level to find the height on the cedar tree that is perfectly level with the screw in the maple tree.

Place a screw in the cedar tree at the height that is level with the screw in the maple tree. If your beam will be held in place with a static uplift arrestor on one end and a dynamic uplift arrestor on the other, you *must* take into account an extra ½ inch for the UHMW piece attached to the dynamic uplift arrestor, which would raise the end of the beam out of level by half an inch. If you're using two dynamic uplift arrestors, the step is not necessary, as the UHMW pieces will raise the beam ends by the same amount.

In this example, we will assume a dynamic uplift arrestor is being used only on the end of the beam attached to the cedar. To account for the height difference, a new screw is placed in the cedar tree exactly half an inch below the screw you already placed. We will drill at the level of the second (lower) screw, so back the first (upper) screw out of the tree.

Step 3: Finding the TAB Orientation

Finding the optimal locations and angles to drill into the trees is a simple matter of understanding how the beam will be positioned. Stretching a string between the trees at the level of the two screws, in the same orientation as the beam you want to install, will show how the beam is oriented in space. The best drilling spot is where the line touches the bark, creating a tangent (Fig. 20). From there, you will try to drill toward the exact center of the tree trunk. Ideally, a TAB should be installed so that it is aimed directly at the center of the tree (Fig. 21).

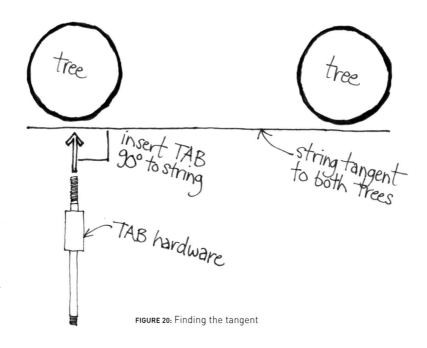

FIGURE 20: Finding the tangent

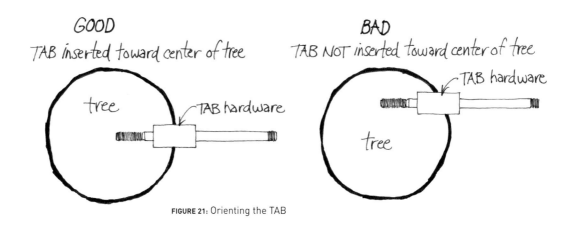

FIGURE 21: Orienting the TAB

Step 4: Drilling

Now that you have taken care to measure the TAB locations and
orientations correctly, drilling holes for the TABs is a straightforward
process. Be sure you are comfortably and securely standing on a
ladder and/or in a harness before starting. It may also be necessary
to place a lanyard around the tree and yourself so that there is
something to push against when the drilling gets tough—and it always
does. The type of drill necessary for the following steps produces a
large amount of torque, and poor footing can be very dangerous.

Remember to *take your time*. The process of drilling takes
several steps, all of which have to be executed with care to ensure a
properly drilled hole, which is crucial for the TAB to function properly.

The way these holes are created will determine the structural integrity of your treehouse, so be sure to spend time making them as exact as possible.

Tip: Rather than drilling all the holes in all the trees first, then inserting the TABs, it's a good idea to drill each hole just before the TAB is inserted. Often, if a drilled hole is left open for more than a few minutes, the moisture from the tree will cause the wood around the hole to swell, and it will be extremely difficult to insert the TAB into the tree.

Step 4.1: The First Bore

Drill the primary hole into the tree using a 1-by-18-inch auger bit while observing the proper orientation you determined in Step 2 (Fig. 22). The 1-inch diameter of the hole is the minor diameter of the 1¼-inch coarse thread and is critical in allowing the thread to bite into the tree. It is also important while you are drilling to keep the drill as level as possible, so periodically place a 9-inch torpedo level directly on the auger bit to be sure the hole is being drilled levelly. For standard 6-by-12-inch TABs, the entire threaded section and half of the boss will penetrate the wood, so the primary hole should be drilled 9 inches beyond the bark. It's important to drill to a precise depth. If the hole is not deep enough, the TAB will not be inserted as far as necessary into the tree, and if it's too deep you'll have an empty space behind the TAB, which isn't good either.

Tip: Before drilling, mark the auger bit at the proper depth by wrapping tape around it, then compensate for the bark once its depth has been determined.

Be sure to sink the boss the required depth into the wood of the tree. This is critical to maintaining the integrity of the treehouse structure. Stay with it and make it happen!

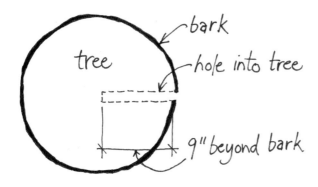

FIGURE 22: The first bore

Step 4.2: Make Room for the Boss

Before a standard TAB can be inserted, you must remove an additional 3-inch-diameter section from the tree to accommodate the boss of the TAB (Fig. 23). Doing this precisely requires a modified 3-inch Forstner bit, commonly used in the plumbing trades to run pipe through wood framing. For the bits we offer through Nelson Treehouse and Supply, we remove the supplied self-feed point and replace it with a custom dummy that fits into the first 1-inch hole. A small tooth on the edge of the dummy cuts the important shoulder where the coarse threads end and the diameter of the round stock jumps back up to 1¼ inches before the boss. This seems trivial, but the engineers assure us that the full inch of 1¼-inch shaft behind the boss, before the thread begins, effectively eliminates a weak point in the TAB's design. We stick the end of this bit into the center of the previously drilled hole and widen the first 3 inches of it (meaning you will only use this bit to drill into the tree 3 inches beyond the bark), which will make room for the boss.

Step 4.3: Clean Up

Remove all the sawdust and wood chips from drilling that may be left inside the hole. We do this by blowing air into the hole through a straw or a short section of the water level's tubing, so we can be sure to get all of the drilling debris out from the back of the hole. This is important, because the TAB will be a very tight fit, and there is no room for wood shavings. It's a good idea to double-check the measurements after drilling to ensure their accuracy and make any necessary adjustments before inserting the TAB.

Patrick drills the 3-inch hole using a modified Forstner bit. Be sure to drill the full 3 inches into the wood, not including the bark.

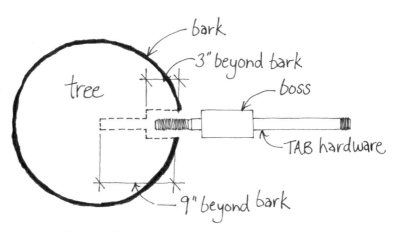

FIGURE 23: The second bore

Step 5: Inserting a TAB

Insert the TAB into the hole and begin screwing it in by hand. Once the boss starts to enter, you will need to switch to a 24-inch pipe wrench. It's a good idea to make a mark on the boss halfway down the length of it, so you can see how far you need to insert it. You should also be able to feel when the boss hits the back of its hole, so if you are in doubt about how far to insert the TAB, just keep turning it until it becomes impossible to go any farther.

Tip: If the TAB is being stubborn before it has bottomed out in its hole and is hard for a single person to turn, try adding some leverage. A 3-foot metal pipe slipped over the handle of the pipe wrench can aid the solo installer. If you have an assistant, a rope can be tied to the end of the wrench handle, and the assistant can tug on the rope from the ground as you turn the wrench. Be sure your ground person has a hard hat on!

Step 6: Placing and Securing the Beams

Once all the TABs have been installed, the beams can be hoisted into place. To do this, first place the beams directly on the TABs, up against the boss, with no uplift arrestors underneath. Position the beam so the edge closest to the tree is up against the boss. Once the beams are correctly positioned, slide the uplift arrestors onto the TABs, lifting the beams slightly in the process, and place the hardware evenly underneath the beam. Once in place, predrill holes in the beams using a ⅜-inch bit, and then secure the hardware in place with ½-by-4-inch galvanized lag bolts.

A skill set that comes in handy when lifting heavy beams into position is rope-and-cable rigging. It is a highly specialized and potentially dangerous trade that will not be delved into in this book. Certified arborists can be hired to assist in this sometimes critical aspect of building a substantial structure aloft. There are also excellent sources of information on the Internet or in books, particularly those by Brion Toss at www.briontoss.com. A good block and tackle, properly set, can be easily mastered and save your back in a big way!

Step 7: Adding the Dynamic Triangle

The dynamic triangle provides even more strength to the beam-to-tree connection by supporting the end of the TAB, and we use it as often as possible. It simply increases the support strength of the TAB, which is always a good idea.

ABOVE: Turn the TAB into the tree using a large pipe wrench, a 24-inch at a minimum. You will know when the TAB is in place.

OPPOSITE: Rigging for treehouse building is a complex and important process. Be sure to do your research before attempting any heavy lifts.

The 4-by-12-inch Douglas fir beam is captured by the hardware, though still allowing tree movement, and ready to receive the floor joist layer.

Step 7.1: The K-nut

The K-nut is the first piece we need to assemble the dynamic triangle. Screw the K-nut onto the exposed threaded end of the TAB. The top of the K-nut (where the turnbuckle will attach) must be pointing upward, which often means it may not be tightened all the way onto the TAB. This is expected. Just be sure that it is tightened as much as possible and is still in the proper orientation.

Step 7.2: Turnbuckle and Whip

To assemble the rest of the dynamic triangle, adjust the turnbuckle so it is extended to roughly three quarters of its maximum length, then attach one jaw of the turnbuckle to the K-nut and the other jaw to the cable sling. The cable sling is ⅜-inch aircraft cable with swaged eye ends. Now pull the free end of the sling toward the tree (above the TAB) until it is taut. Mark the spot where the eye of the sling touches the tree.

Step 7.3: Drilling for the Lag Bolt

On the spot you have marked, drill a hole into the tree using a ¾-inch-diameter auger bit (the minor diameter of a 1-inch lag bolt). This hole should be drilled straight into the tree, perpendicular to the outstretched sling and aimed directly toward the center of the tree. Be sure to only drill deep enough to accommodate the 1-by-8-inch galvanized lag bolt, leaving about 2 inches outside of the bark (less, if the bark is particularly thick).

Step 7.4: Installing Lag and Removing Slack

Place the 1-inch lag bolt through the eye of the sling, then screw it into the hole until the eye of the sling is against the tree. Lastly, tighten the turnbuckle until it is hand-tight.

Safety First

Before going any further, it is time for a safety meeting.

Seriously.

Initially, this means clearing the base of the tree of fallen branches and debris, placing safety lines high in the trees, and setting some basic ground rules. No work site is ever 100 percent safe, but there are several things you can do to minimize the risk of injury to everyone on and around the site.

Make it absolutely clear to everyone on the site that walking under the tree is forbidden during construction. I recommend requiring hard hats for everyone near the perimeter of the tree. If there are kids around, under no circumstances should they be allowed close to the building area while work is going on. Between the dangerous tools and possible falling objects, it's just too risky. If you want to include them, find off-site tasks to keep them busy and contributing. It might be simply sinking star-drive screws into a log and then removing them until they get the hang of it. It's never too early to start training new treehouse builders.

Whenever anyone is in the tree on an open platform, they've got to be attached properly to a safety line with a climbing harness. This is the most important rule and it must be strongly enforced. Basic information on how to do this is coming up.

The Garlic Ceremony

Before we set any lines in the tree, we like to take a moment and let the trees know that we come in peace. That probably sounds a little crazy, but it makes us feel good, and hopefully the trees too. We usually say a few words, ask permission, promise to be careful and treat the trees with respect. They are our hosts, after all, and we would like nothing more than to live in harmony with them. Finally, we bury a clove of garlic at the base of each tree to ward off disease and evil spirits, and then we let it rip!

Static Safety Lines and the Prusik Knot

Setting a safety line is the first order of business as you move into the trees. It is the most important element of a safe building site, so if you don't already have the gear, invest in a quality rope and climbing harness right away. Gear shopping is always a pleasure, so why not throw in a good rock-climbing helmet while you are at it, and a few carabiners as well? It is easy to get carried away with all the fancy climbing gear that is available today, but we can keep it simple, too. Depending on the size of the building crew and the configuration of the trees, you may need multiple safety lines. The way to attach to them is with a simple Prusik knot made from a length of ½-inch climbing rope (Fig. 24).

Setting the static safety line to begin with can be a little tricky. We often use a Big Shot slingshot, which can be ordered online, to shoot a 12-ounce weighted bag with a light nylon throw line attached high into the tree canopy. It takes a few attempts, typically, and you want to be sure to aim for a sturdy crotch or major branch. Once you make it, pull the heavier climbing rope up and over, then anchor the end to the trunk of a sturdy neighboring tree. A classic bowline knot will come in handy for this anchoring knot (Fig. 25). Call in an arborist if you are the least bit uncomfortable in setting these first lines. From this point on, anyone on the platform during construction is required to tie off to a safety line with a Prusik knot hooked independently to their rock-climbing harness with a locking carabiner.

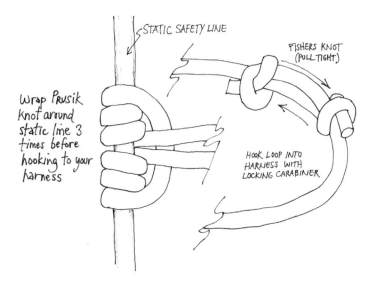

STATIC SAFETY LINE

FISHERS KNOT
(PULL TIGHT)

Wrap Prusik knot around static line 3 times before hooking to your harness

HOOK LOOP INTO HARNESS WITH LOCKING CARABINER

FIGURE 24: The Prusik knot

The Bowline Knot

Here is the knot where the rabbit comes out of the hole, goes around the tree, and goes back in the hole. It is a simple and essential knot that is easy to tie, can take a huge strain, and unties easily.

FIGURE 25: The bowline knot

Building Your Treehouse

With a sturdy platform installed and ready to go, it is time to shift your thinking to the shell of the treehouse. As this area of the building could be the sole subject of a different book, I will not go too deeply into it, except to offer the following tips.

Wood-frame construction is the only way to go. It is light, strong, and flexible. Books and information on "stick-frame construction" abound, so if you are not familiar with how to frame the shell of a building, put this research project on your priority list. Framing a treehouse can be simple or infinitely complex—you decide. Either way, framing is fun and enormously satisfying, as it can happen quickly and give the project positive momentum.

Frame your treehouse using the latest battery-powered screwdrivers and a big box of 3-inch "star drive" self-tapping screws. No need for nail guns, air compressors, or air hoses. If you make a mistake, simply back the screw out and fix it!

Take advantage of your platform. If you have a nice flat surface up in the tree with room to lay out and frame your walls, go for it. This will save you the struggle of lifting wall sections up from below.

Your building plan should have an access plan. There are many ways to enter a treehouse, but the most common way is by stairs. Ladders, bridges, and elevators can be awfully fun, but a good set of stairs is hard to beat. Don't let them psych you out! They may seem complicated, but a simple set is actually quite easy to build. I recommend breaking a typical run of 10 to 15 feet of elevation gain into two sections. The first stair section will be ridged to the ground and rise to an ample landing perhaps two-thirds of the way up to the treehouse floor level. The second stair section will need to be flexible and move, as the trees move the platform in the wind. I secure the top of this stair section to the platform in a meaningful way. Overdo it, in other words. Then use some of the same UHMW plastic that is used as a friction plate in the dynamic uplift arrestor on the surface of the landing where the base of the second stair section lands. This is an important decoupling that will ensure the safety and longevity of your stairway into the trees.

A question I am often asked is how long a treehouse can last. The answer is that a treehouse can last as long as the trees themselves. Good design and construction techniques combined with normal home maintenance will ensure a long life for any treehouse. Technically, that means if you build in a bristlecone pine, and maybe fund a foundation to maintain your creation, your treehouse could last for 6,000 years!

Planning and Permitting, or What I Learned the Hard Way from Treehouse Point

Good planning is essential for a successful treehouse project. It starts with a detailed building plan and covers the sometimes unpleasant business of dealing with your local building authority. Turning a blind eye to these people can land you in some serious hot water.

Each of us has our own reasons for doing things the way we do, and I am not one to judge. At Treehouse Point, a commercial endeavor, I began by building first and filing for permits later, which was the only way I thought possible. Perhaps I was right, but it exacted a price that is difficult to quantify. Permitting after the fact was paid for in blood, sweat, and tears. Many tears. And money. The money part arrives early in the process and lasts throughout.

The price of going about planning piecemeal is high as well. It is paid up front and continuously along the way. The difficulty for me was in knowing what a long-term plan might look like in a venture as malleable as Treehouse Point. In King County, Washington, once it was discovered that I was building a treehouse within the 165-foot buffer to the salmon-bearing Raging River, the order came to tear my treehouse down or they would do it for me. And encumber the property with a lien to pay for the task.

Strong words via certified mail.

It's the kind of thing that can lead to poor health.

A lasting lesson for me is that the authorities in charge of keeping us all safe from ourselves never go away. They are open to considering new ideas, but treehouse builders need to work hard to receive their blessings. There are parts of our great country where we have done away with building inspectors, but in my corner of the world, they rule. My advice: Plan accordingly.

If the answer to any of the following questions is "yes," you should speak to your local building authorities before you start to build your treehouse.

1. Are you planning to use the treehouse for commercial purposes?
2. Will the treehouse in any way be a nuisance to your neighbors? Obstructing views, invading privacy, creating noise issues?
3. Will the treehouse be in violation of any neighborhood covenants, deeds, or restrictions?
4. Is the structure going to be within any front yard, side yard, or rear yard building setbacks?
5. Will it be within any so-called "critical area" setbacks and buffers from steep slopes, wildlife corridors, or riparian boundaries (lakes, rivers, oceans)?

6. Is there anything in the local building code that addresses "tree-supported structures"?
7. Is there a building height limit? Often it is 30 to 35 feet from average ground level to the top of the roof.

And even if everything appears to be a go, my strong recommendation would be then to go speak with any neighbors who would be even remotely affected. Let them know your plan. It could save unnecessary headaches in the long run and improve neighbor relations immediately. By the way, it makes no difference for building permits if the building will have plumbing or electricity. Those are both separate permits, typically. I do recommend that those permits be obtained even if you choose not to get a permit for the treehouse itself.

Here is a step-by-step guide to what it takes to get a treehouse through a typical building permit process:

Basic Necessities for Obtaining a Building Permit

1. Show the precise location of the treehouse on a plot plan of your property. You may need to involve a surveyor if the local tax assessor's maps are inadequate. Be sure to indicate all the applicable setbacks on the plot plan, and know that if the treehouse is placed within the setbacks, then a new level of planning and unpredictability will kick into effect: the "variance" process.
2. Draw the treehouse plan to scale in detail, including platform layout with beam and joist sizes, a floor plan, at least two elevation drawings, and a section—this is a look through the structure as if it were cut in half, detailing wall, floor, and roof thicknesses. These are the structural bones of the project.
3. Prepare a detailed plan of the connections to the tree(s) and the ground, if applicable. Most likely a registered structural engineer will need to sign off on the connections. Go to the website www.treehouseengineering.com for inspiration here. Hopefully a local engineer will get the picture well enough to sign off on the information provided; otherwise you may need to get in line for Charley Greenwood himself. Charley has been the treehouse industry's go-to guy for twenty years. He is brilliant and busy. Another contact is Nabil Taha in Klamath Falls, Oregon (licensed in most states), or Ben Brungraber in Massachusetts. Or better yet, maybe you are an engineer yourself!
4. The process of applying for a building permit varies, so call ahead and see what they say. Then be ready to start writing checks.

There you have it.
I'm sorry.

3 Putting It All Together: The WC Ranch Treehouse

The WC Ranch, outside of Merrill, Oregon, came into existence in 1969, when my wife, Judy, and her family moved up from Los Angeles. I arrived there for the first time in 1982, having grown up in densely populated suburban New Jersey, and I was stunned by its natural beauty.

We were married there in 1986, exactly where the stairs land at the new treehouse in the sacred place we call Ellen's garden.

A few years ago, Nancy, my mother-in-law, took me aside and claimed that she was ready. "For what?" I wondered. Maybe this was going to be the pep talk for me to get a proper career outside of treehouse building. Instead, with an excited twinkle in her eye, she said that she would like to surprise the family with a treehouse. I must admit that I felt some pressure. Nancy has always supported our unconventional career choice, and for that simple bit of grace I wanted to build her something wonderful. Walls of cedar shingle were her only request, so I designed something to match her classic and timeless style. The following spring, our newly formed company, Nelson Treehouse and Supply, sent the crew and put all hands on deck to create this special arboreal guesthouse that has every family member fighting for reservations.

Our crew consisted of five carpenters and countless family members and volunteers. We spent about a week prefabricating the walls and roof in the comfort of our shop in Fall City, Washington, and then about ten days assembling and finishing everything on-site.

PREVIOUS PAGE: When I was eight years old, I had the deep privilege of being the youngest member of the Trappers and Explorers' Club in Brookhaven, New York. We were four members in total. Our clubhouse was a disheveled garden shed with beautiful lines. Even an eight-year-old could see this. When Nancy DeFeyeter, my mother-in-law, asked me to build her treehouse, I resorted to the roots of my aesthetic. The Trappers and Explorers' Club house rose again.

LEFT: Judy and I were married just a few steps to the right of this photograph, on the original stone entrance of a house that once stood here. Siberian elms hold a new house. They grow just outside the remaining perimeter of the bygone home's stone foundation.

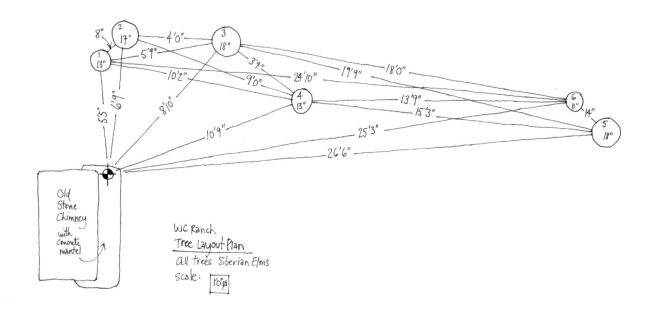

WC Ranch
Tree Layout Plan
All trees Siberian Elms
Scale: 1'0"ø

Old Stone Chimney with concrete mantel

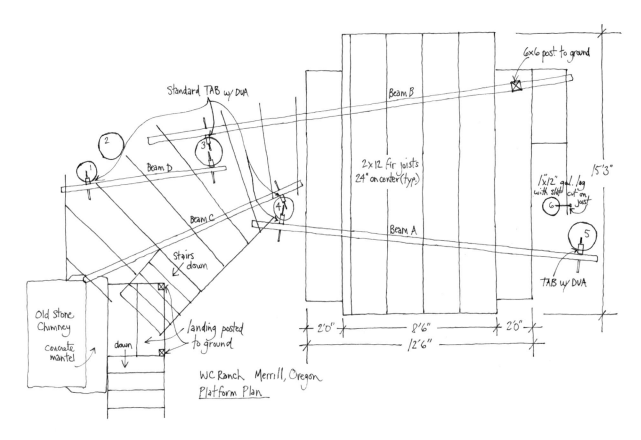

Standard TAB w/ DUA

Beam B

Beam D

6x6 post to ground

2x12 fir joists 24" on center (typ.)

Beam C

1"x12" gal. lag with slot cut on joist

Beam A

Stairs down

TAB w/ DUA

landing posted to ground

Old Stone Chimney

Concrete mantel

down

2'0"   8'6"   2'0"

12'6"

15'3"

WC Ranch   Merrill, Oregon
Platform Plan

This is a representation of the four phases of drawing a treehouse plan. It starts with a scaled tree layout plan. Then, a platform plan is refined *after* a few passes at the floor plan. And finally, elevations are drawn.

The elevations can be *anything*! If your treehouse needs to be a classic single style—so be it. If it needs to be Frank Gehry—make it so! If it is something no one has ever seen before—more power to you. Just do it!

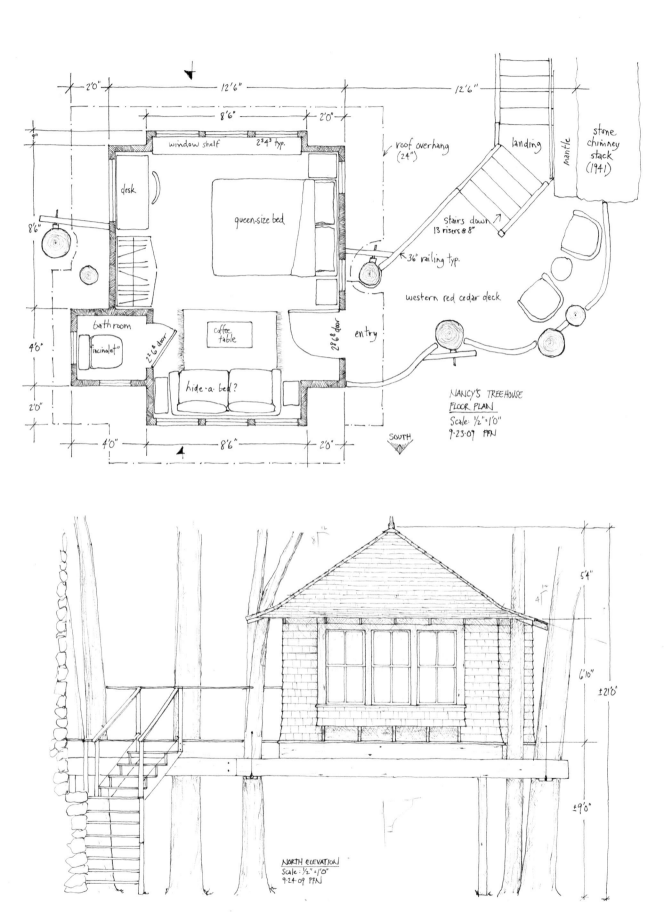

2'0" · **12'6"** · **12'6"**

9"

window shelf   2'4³ typ.   **8'6"** · **2'0"**

desk

queen-size bed

8'6"

↙ roof overhang (24")

landing

mantle

stone chimney stack (1941)

stairs down ↖
13 risers @ 8"

← 36" railing typ.

western red cedar deck

bathroom

"incinolet"

2'6" door

coffee table

2'8" door

entry

hide-a-bed?

NANCY'S TREEHOUSE
FLOOR PLAN
Scale: ½"=1'0"
9-23-09 PFN

4'0"

2'0"

4'0" · **8'6"** · **2'0"**

SOUTH

5'4"

6'10"

±21'0"

±9'0"

NORTH ELEVATION
Scale: ½"=1'0"
9-24-09 PFN

ABOVE LEFT: Adjustments were made where a tree was not behaving according to plan.

BELOW LEFT: Ian Weedman turns in a 1-by-8-inch galvanized lag screw that anchors the top of the cable suspender.

ABOVE RIGHT: A 6-inch screw is placed about 3 inches above the drilling point to indicate the left/right orientation of the TAB. A short torpedo level placed directly on the 1-inch ship auger will guide the up/down orientation of the first boring.

BELOW RIGHT: One method of insulating a treehouse floor is to drop in plywood soffit panels and R30 fiberglass batt insulation before a ¾-inch plywood subfloor is applied to the top of the joists.

ABOVE: The old chimney serves as a static attachment point for the deck portion of the treehouse plan.

BELOW LEFT: The floor insulation method chosen here allows easy movement between the beam and joist level. Insulating your floor is critical in cold environments, as this is the part most vulnerable to cold infiltration.

BELOW RIGHT: Ian and Daryl McDonald unload the prefabricated wall parts of the treehouse. Typically we prefabricate all of our walls in our home shop in Fall City, Washington, to limit the time spent on the road.

ABOVE: The walls are designed so that two to four people can lift them easily into place. Once the walls have been raised, the precut roof rafters are installed.

BELOW: Many things can occur simultaneously once the shell and the frame are in place. My brother-in-law, Monnie Hedges, contemplates the window openings and hopes they were framed to the correct size.

ABOVE: Daryl is always given the trickier tasks. In this case he is making adjustments to the roof where one of the Siberian elms is closer to the structure than we bargained for.

BELOW: A serendipitous visit from one of my European building partners, Christopher Richter, and his nephew, Dominic, allowed us to subcontract the roof sheathing to a capable duo.

ABOVE: Erecting strong scaffolding out of two-by-fours and ½-inch plywood around the perimeter of any treehouse project is well worth the time it takes to install it. Make it strong and make your life ten times easier.

BELOW: Chuck McClellan spent a good deal of time and brainpower building an elegant stairway.

ABOVE LEFT: Charlie Nelson expertly weaves a corner with perfection-grade western red cedar shingles, while Daryl starts the first course of shingles on the roof.

ABOVE RIGHT: Rookie carpenter and family member Kevin O'Brien does his best to follow the line in a crucial finish cut.

BELOW: The railings stop short of the trees so the trees can move in the wind. Here I am filling in some larger gaps with juniper branches that were harvested just a few steps away.

ABOVE: When looking back at the treehouse from the alfalfa fields, Stukel Mountain rises majestically in the background.

BELOW: Treehouses have a way of uniting friends and family like nothing else. Now, in this sacred place named for a lost family member, Ellen's garden, we forever have a reminder of the ten great days we spent together.

ABOVE: A recommended interior for any treehouse is 1-by-6-inch tongue-and-groove wood paneling—here, we used remilled Douglas fir. In any case, avoid plaster and Sheetrock, as it they do not flex like wood does.

BELOW: A supremely comfortable bed awaits family members, who have to reserve the special guest room well in advance.

A Tour of Single-tree Designs

Now let's have a look at a diverse group of treehouses that have one thing in common: a single supporting tree. There are many ways to approach this seemingly simple design challenge, and the projects that follow represent solutions that our company created over the past several years.

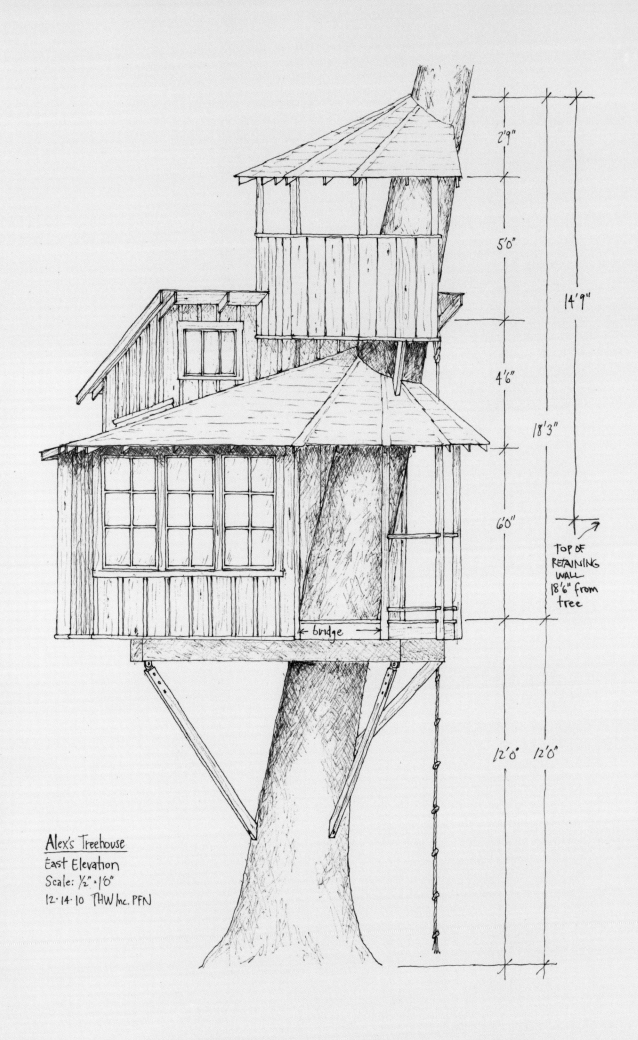

2'9"

5'0"

14'9"

4'6"

18'3"

6'0"

TOP OF
RETAINING
WALL
18'6" from
tree

bridge

12'0" 12'0"

Alex's Treehouse
East Elevation
Scale: 1/2" = 1'0"
12·14·10 THW Inc. PFN

John and Alex's Serious Treehouse

Washington State

Finding a tree large enough to support a treehouse on its own can be a challenge in its own right. How you go about supporting the treehouse once you do is a challenge of a different kind. In fact, there are many ways to build in single trees. We reviewed earlier the "6 feet off the bark" limitations of the paddle TAB and knee brace method, and then touched on the Roman cross method for larger loads. This is an example of a very large load on a Roman cross system.

Alex's Graffiti Studio

Mid-Atlantic States

Young Alex needed a place to develop his budding interest in graffiti art. It was our honor to build him this single-tree design in a stunning London plane tree. The prominent location of the tree necessitated a building permit, and engineer Charley Greenwood gave us our first taste of an entirely steel substructure. It was only with this advanced design that we were able to convince the powers that be that Alex would be safe in his sylvan studio. This modest foray into steel construction, which we built for a young artist searching for his muse, was the inspiration for a more ambitious feat of engineering: the Burl at Treehouse Point (p. 35).

OPPOSITE: Steel knee braces support a multilevel art studio nestled in an urban forest.

ABOVE LEFT: A cedar ladder leads up along the trunk and through the skip sheeting of the roof system to the ultimate lookout.

ABOVE RIGHT: A rope bridge stretches 20 feet across a chasm to the beckoning entrance.

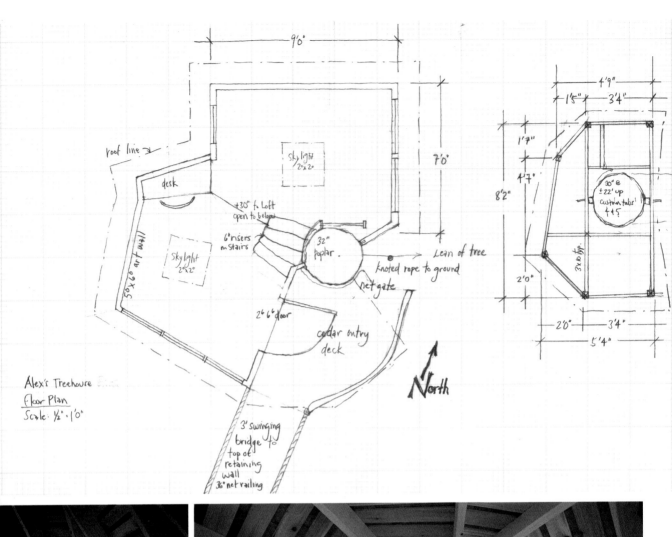

roof line

desk

Sky light
2'0 x 2'0

Skylight
2'0 x 2'0

5'0 x 6'0 art wall

+30" to Loft
open to below

6" risers
m stairs

32"
poplar

Lean of tree

Knoted rope to ground

net gate

2'6" door

cedar entry
deck

3' swinging
bridge to
top of
retaining
wall
36" net railing

North

Alex's Treehouse
Floor Plan
Scale: ½" · 1'0"

9'0"

7'0"

4'9"

1'5"   3'4"

1'7"

4'7"

8'2"

30" Ø
± 22' up
custom tabs!
+5

3 x 10 typ.

2'0"

2'0"   3'4"

5'4"

ABOVE LEFT: A 360-degree view awaits the adventurous from the lookout.

ABOVE RIGHT: A critical consideration in any roof frame is keeping the framing a healthy distance off the bark of the trunk to allow for tree growth.

OPPOSITE: The multilevel studio required intense engineering to pass through a strict city building department.

Cottage Lake Treehouse

Washington State

This wonderful lakefront treehouse came about from a visit that the clients made to Treehouse Point, our bed-and-breakfast. I was proud to hear that when the Shephards emerged from their night in a treehouse, my son Charlie happened to be walking by. They asked how the trees respond to the load of a house, and he said, "The trees love it!" I couldn't agree more.

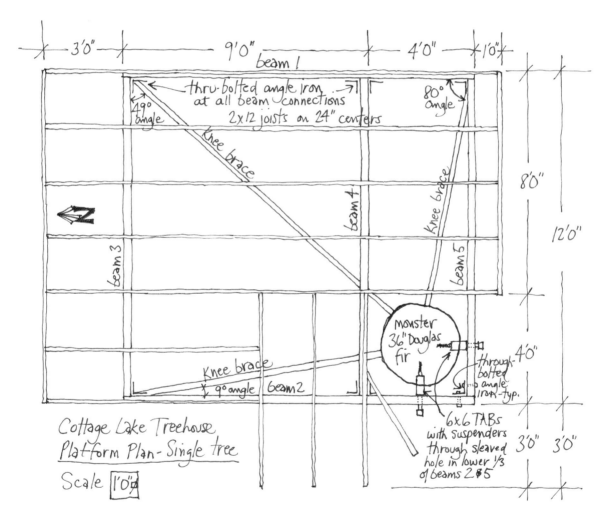

Cottage Lake Treehouse
Platform Plan - Single tree
Scale 1'0"

Beam and joist detail labels: 3'0", 9'0" beam 1, 4'0", 1'0"
thru-bolted angle iron at all beam connections
2x12 joists on 24" centers
49° angle, 80° angle
Knee brace, beam 4, beam 5
8'0", 12'0"
beam 3, N
Knee brace, 9° angle, beam 2
monster 36" Douglas fir
through-bolted angle iron - typ.
4'0", 3'0", 3'0"
6x6 TABs with suspenders through sleaved hole in lower 1/3 of beams 2 & 5

OPPOSITE: This single-tree design is unique in that the tree's position is at the corner of a 12-by-17-foot rectangle. The massive beam and knee brace substructure supports an even larger cantilevered floor joist system that rests above.

ABOVE: Many times during the building of this treehouse, I would look out over the 60-acre lake and see a family of bald eagles circling above in the autumn sun. We lucked out when the building inspector circled around and decided this nest was well built and not something that we would disturb.

The Witch House

Ibiza, Spain

The great theologian Joseph Campbell taught us to follow our bliss. I took his advice starting in the late 1980s, and one manifestation of this was a phone call from a man on a famous party island off of the Spanish mainland. Joerg needed a treehouse for his young son, Daniel, and wondered if I could coach him long-distance. I told him that for a reasonable fee he could have me and even my wife, Judy, come to show him how to build his treehouse personally. He agreed to this most excellent idea, and as Joseph Campbell foretold, if one follows one's bliss, wonderful things ensue.

Ivona, Joerg's wife, treated Judy like a long-lost sister, and though I never had a chance to get down to the beach, I made friends that I will treasure for the rest of my life.

ABOVE: The underside of Daniel's treehouse was concealed with the bark of the cedars that we used for siding.

OPPOSITE: An Aleppo pine hosts an eclectic creation using locally sourced materials. The round windows were built on-site after I left the island by a talented mason turned carpenter, Bartosz Sikorski.

OPPOSITE: The inside of the Witch House was trimmed with short lengths of local olive wood. Aleppo pine branch roof rafters were harvested on-site.

ABOVE LEFT: After we worked together for two weeks, Bartosz, the mason, trained himself in the fine art of interior-finish carpentry. He did a wonderful job.

ABOVE RIGHT: Bartosz's folksy portal window captures the essence of a hand-built house.

BELOW LEFT: A network of branches and stair treads winds around the Aleppo pine, creating a sturdy and eclectic entryway.

BELOW RIGHT: The branch work continues to the entry platform and defines the spirit of the entire project.

The Spirit House

Rhinebeck, New York

When you think you're out of luck and no trees are jumping out at you, don't worry. Keep the faith. Keep looking. Look closer. Open your mind. All we are really trying to do is get close to the trees. Why not fit something up against the trees? Use a post or two to take the pressure off, and make something happen.

That is exactly what we did outside of Rhinebeck, New York, on an old farm property that was looking a little worse for wear. The new owner of the weekend getaway decided to build a small arboreal retreat before she dug into the longer-term project of restoring the original farmhouse.

That's good thinking, in my book.

LEFT: The inside of the Spirit House was designed for inspiration. The owner is an author and is excited to use the treehouse as a muse.

OPPOSITE: Inspired by Thai spirit houses, the cedar-wood filigree was lifted from a photograph that the owner sent to me. Most of the detail is in gold leaf.

The Irish Cottage

Huntington Beach, California

When I posed the question to Chris and Nicole Pittman-Staab after an enthusiastic treehouse site visit to their home in Southern California, I was surprised by their willingness to participate in our TV experiment. I am grateful that they did. Nicole and Chris became Episode 2 in Season 1 of *Treehouse Masters*, and tears of joy were captured on the last day of filming—TV gold, so I'm told. I'm still a little embarrassed.

Finding the tree was easy. It was the only tree in the tightly confined backyard.

But oh, what a beauty she is! An ancient olive, and a remnant of what might have been a beautiful grove before the houses came.

As beautiful and strong as the olive is, the program for the desired space exceeded the tree's size and strength. It was determined that this would be a house mainly supported at the perimeter by posts to the ground, but with one central support landing directly on the old tree's trunk. The trick was going to be how to fit the house in the tree without cutting too many of its branches.

OPPOSITE: A nautilus-shaped structure floats above an ancient olive tree and serves as a place for the owners to remember their Irish heritage.

ABOVE: Scaffolding still in place shows the joyful challenge of building in tight spaces.

The Pittman-Staabs have a deep affinity for all things Irish. And part of the deal was that Nicole really wanted the exterior to be black fieldstone in the style of an old Irish cottage. But in a tree?

No could do. Especially in Seismic Zone 4.

But I love the solution: a broken pattern of western red cedar shingles that mimic the look of fieldstone. Shingles are one of my favorite materials to work with; they look wonderful, and when installed properly they can last a lifetime.

If you blur your vision, I think it works!

ABOVE: A peat-burning fireplace anchors the center of the oddly shaped interior. Cork walls painted shades of Irish green remind the owners of a land they love.

OPPOSITE: Nicole's father's chair sits quietly in a rare corner of the round house.

A Tour of Multiple-tree Designs

Now we can look at a selection of multi-tree projects that we have built over the past several years. It is rare to find four trees spaced just the right distances apart to allow for a quick and easy two-beam platform, but it happens. More likely, a creative beam-and-joist configuration awaits in a two-to-five-or-more-tree scenario.

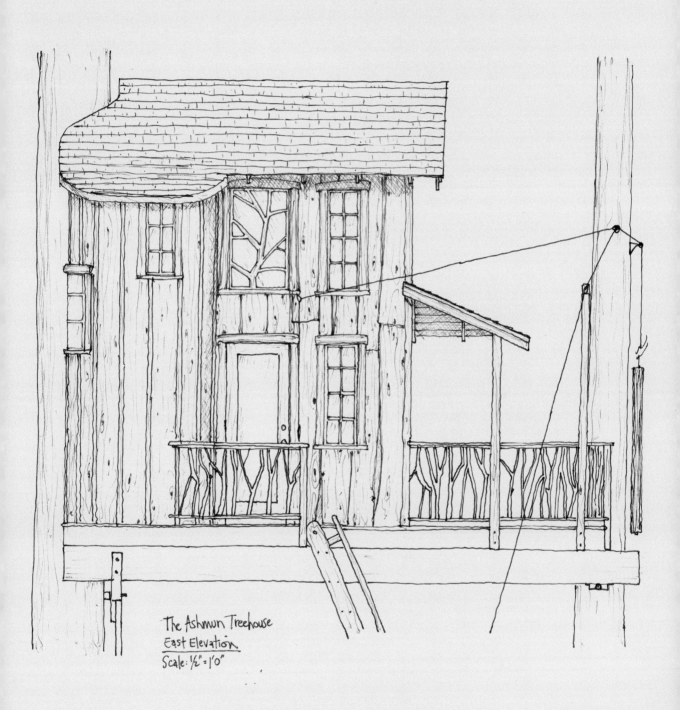

The Ashmun Treehouse
East Elevation
Scale: ½" = 1'0"

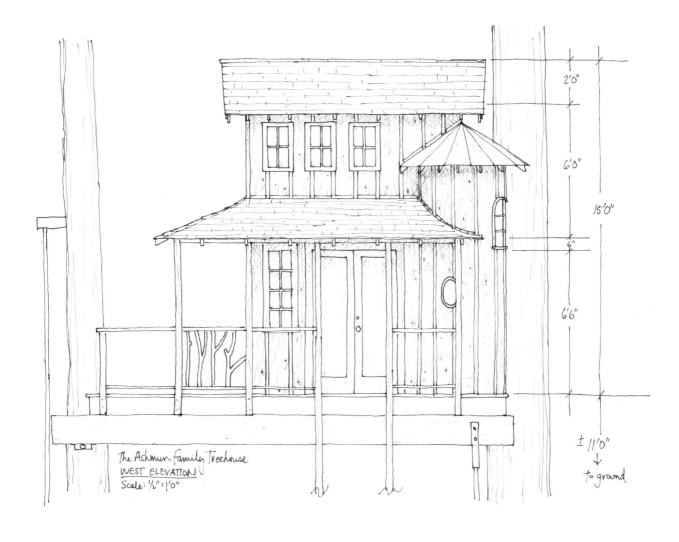

The Ashmun family Treehouse
WEST ELEVATION
Scale: ½" = 1'0"

2'0"

6'0"

15'0"

6"

6'6"

± 11'0"
↓
to ground

Highland

Seattle, Washington

This treehouse straddles a mature Douglas fir and a specimen Seattle sequoia. The floor and platform structure needed to be high enough to allow vehicles to pass under and access other parts of the property. Two separate round towers were a nice challenge for us to build, and aside from heavy snowfall halfway through the building process, it all went off without a hitch. Although it is primarily a children's playhouse and overnight camp, a hosted dinner in this two-story hideaway is sometimes auctioned off at an annual fund-raiser for the local school.

OPPOSITE: The two-story playhouse starts 14 feet above terra firma. It provides fertile ground for a child's boundless imagination.

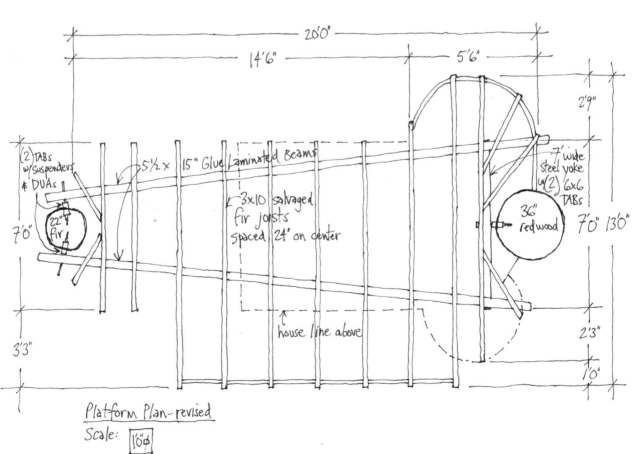

Platform Plan - revised
Scale: 1'0"⌀

20'0"

14'6"

5'6"

2'9"

(2) TABs w/suspenders & DUAs

5½ x 15" Glue Laminated Beams

3x10 salvaged fir joists spaced 24" on center

7' wide steel yoke w/(2) 6x6 TABs

7'0"

22"⌀ fir

36" redwood

7'0" 13'0"

house line above

3'3"

2'3"

1'0"

OPPOSITE ABOVE: The east tower appears to cantilever precariously over a 5½-by-15-inch glue-laminated beam.

ABOVE: When a specimen redwood tree such as this one grows north of Seattle, I make an exception to the rule that trees should not penetrate the envelop of a building. In this case the trunk, with its beautiful reddish brown bark, makes up a significant portion of one wall on the first floor. The connection between the structure and the tree has a flexible gasket made of durable black fabric. This will allow for tree growth more than movement in the wind.

BELOW: Upstairs, bunk beds expand the playhouse into an overnight camp. The big branch window was built by sandwiching the glass between two pieces of cut-out cedar.

The White (Oak) House and Mooney Brewhouse

Glenmont, Ohio

At the Mohican Resort in Glenmont, Ohio, we, along with some excellent local Amish carpenters, had the privilege to build not one but two unusual treehouses. The first spanned five mature white oaks and is a completely self-contained guesthouse. There is a full bathroom—with an adjacent outdoor shower to boot—a kitchen, a living room, a separate bedroom with a queen-size bed, and a sleeping loft with four twin mattresses.

A few hundred yards away we added a second treehouse with a slightly different use—it's a brewery and tasting room. We made the railing a little higher and stronger than usual.

A 40-foot bridge makes the brewhouse even more special (and challenging for beer drinkers). It stretches between a 22-inch white oak and a 24-inch black oak—two beautiful mature trees that can easily bear the weight. Bridges of this length are extremely vulnerable to stresses and must be carefully engineered. The method we used here is a good system that goes up relatively quickly. We used pressure-treated materials in the hopes of keeping maintenance down over the long haul.

OPPOSITE: Handcrafted cedar doors welcome friends and guests to the White (Oak) treehouse in Ohio.

ABOVE: Six trees, mainly white oaks, support a fully equipped guesthouse complete with kitchen, bath, and outside shower.

OVERLEAF: The interior shows the high-quality craftsmanship of the local Amish carpenters and the sharp eye for interior design of Laura Mooney.

ABOVE LEFT: An elephant-proof bridge stretches 40 feet from one sturdy oak to another, welcoming the thirsty traveler.

BELOW LEFT: A steel yoke with a 7-foot spread holds two 16-inch-deep glue-laminated beams far off the trunk of a second black oak.

RIGHT: A gorgeous gothic window, custom built by Ian Franks, is the focal point of this Amish barn–inspired brewhouse. And, as any brewhouse must have, a small washroom sits outside to the left.

OVERLEAF: The interior was quickly assembled by a talented team, led by designer Tory Jones, for the *Treehouse Master* television series.

A classic three-tree scenario of post oaks yielded a perfect space for a 13-by-17-foot Texas spa.

FRONT ELEVATION
Scale: ½"=1'0"
Monica's Spa Treehouse
Austin, TX
NTS · PFN · 11·25·12

Treehouse Spa

Bastrop, Texas

A spa in a treehouse seems a natural fit. Add a place within to spend the night and you are pulling double-duty. At the Davis Ranch Retreat, Monica Davis's 200-square-foot oak-bound oasis is doing just that. It is occupied during the day by a technician offering everything from massages to manicures, and fought over by night as a queen-size place to doze and dream. There is even a full bathroom with a state-of-the-art steam shower.

Ms. Davis runs an advertising placement agency in Austin, Texas, and someone in her camp suggested that she respond to a casting call for a treehouse-based reality show. She had talked wistfully in the office about adding a treehouse to the ranch retreat at her country home, so the subject did not come out of the blue. After a vetting by the higher-ups at Animal Planet, I was given my orders to go see if her trees would be suitable.

Were they ever! In the end we found three strong post oaks arranged in a triangular pattern, 14 feet on two sides and almost 9 feet on the third. It was the perfect situation for a yoke to spread the load.

ABOVE: As Monica's clientele are older and wiser, stairs have been eliminated, and a gradual ramp carries them effortlessly from the pool area into the spa.

OPPOSITE: A small, luxuriously outfitted bath, replete with a steam shower, completes the spa.

BELOW: When the massage table is put away, a Murphy bed lowers from the north wall and allows for use of the treehouse as overnight accommodations.

Jack's Treehouse

Near Seattle, Washington

Jack really is about the luckiest thirteen-year-old in the world. First, he has the greatest parents a kid could ever ask for, and now he has the finest teen hangout a young man could ever imagine. He does have to share it on Sundays, however. The secondary use for the treetop bungalow is serious Seahawks football watching. The long bar is not merely a soda fountain for kids, in the end.

OPPOSITE: Jack's treehouse borrows its lines from the ultimate bungalows built by Greene and Greene in California about a hundred years ago. It is 12 feet off the ground, has 500 square feet of interior floor space on two floors, and weighs 77,000 pounds.

ABOVE: There are two ways into the treehouse: by zip line, or by cabled bridge.

BELOW: The long cedar bar top is the centerpiece of the entertainment room. A full bathroom fits behind the flat-screen TV and a loft that sleeps four lies above.

Valley View

Southern Oregon

Not every treehouse comes together as smoothly as one would like. In this case in southern Oregon, we battled steep terrain, sweltering summertime temperatures, and a reality-show camera crew that was filming the pilot for *Treehouse Masters* and seemingly looking for a fight. The treehouse itself was hard enough to master, and while tempers never blew up, the construction budget did, and many valuable lessons were learned and relearned along the way.

Building treehouses for a profit, like any construction business, is tricky. The larger the project, the more there is to keep track of, and the more crucial a role communication plays. A backyard tree fort is a different animal than, in this case, a fully functional guesthouse supported by six posts and two modest white oaks. The greatest lesson learned in this build was that material specifications and

ABOVE: The back deck is made of western red cedar and locally obtained redwood. White oaks and madrona trees abound in the picturesque Oregon valley.

OPPOSITE: This perspective depicts the steepness of the site. Broad windows in the main bedroom look out over the same idyllic view as the deck.

finished carpentry details must be communicated clearly to both the carpenters and the clients. It is easy to get carried away—especially when you want to show off for television—and forget that time is money.

And money doesn't grow on trees.

And you should tell your client that things are getting a little carried away.

But maybe do that before you get carried away.

Or don't get carried away.

You see? Communication is everything.

Lesson relearned.

We could not have asked for a more scenic setting or a more determined client to see a difficult build through to a successful finish. The "pilot" turned into Episode 6 of the *Treehouse Masters* television show.

ABOVE: A madrona tree—one of my favorite Northwest natives—frames the entry to the well-appointed guesthouse in the trees.

BELOW: A 400-foot boardwalk connects the treehouse to the main house, which stands 300 feet away and 30 feet higher up the steep hillside.

ABOVE: The circular breakfast nook also serves as the centerpiece for fun and conversation.

BELOW: Looking down from the loft above reveals a multipurpose great room. To the right is a small kitchenette and full bathroom. The ladder hanging horizontally above the second bunk was the access ladder to the owner's childhood treehouse, just a few miles away.

The Hackberry Farmhouse

Mart, Texas

A sweeter family I could never ask for. And there were a lot of them to go around! Sandy and Jimmy Maddox decided they could no longer fit in the otherwise ample farmhouse that they had built only ten years before. Of course, I was happy to oblige their desire to expand into the old hackberry trees that had framed the long-gone original homestead.

OPPOSITE: A new house rises in the location of the original homestead.

ABOVE: At the treehouse entrance a massive hackberry tree attempts to obstruct passage to the large, west-facing cocktail deck. However, it does not prevent children from passing.

BELOW: The many Maddox dogs get to share what may be the first treehouse doghouse in all of the great state of Texas.

OVERLEAF: Designer extraordinaire Tory Jones was brought in to outfit the Maddox family clubhouse. She used designer furnishings to brighten both the interior and exterior.

Hidden Hollow Treehouse

Sandwich, Massachusetts

In 2009, the difficult economy made any phone call for a treehouse welcome news, and I leapt at the chance to fly to Boston to cultivate something promising. The Heritage Museum & Gardens in Sandwich, Massachusetts, were kicking around an idea to create an interactive outdoor educational program for children, and a treehouse would be its centerpiece.

The museum's director and I had a joyful time designing and redesigning a structure that had its roots in Scandinavia and its sensibility in Cape Cod. In the end, it was decided that building something so fanciful when so many people were struggling would send the wrong message.

Two years later, however, the Upper Cape Cod Regional Technical School, led by stellar teacher Kevin McFadyen, landed the construction contract, and a heartwarming story ensued. Some twenty-five students, mostly juniors and seniors, worked for two school years, donating roughly 2,500 hours of labor to faithfully complete the plan. It was hardly a full-time project, but according to everyone, the young carpenters thoroughly enjoyed themselves. They did a beautiful job as well.

BELOW LEFT: The Hidden Hollow overlooks a common Cape Cod kettle hole, created by retreating glaciers of the last ice age.

BELOW RIGHT: The churchlike roofline is borrowed from the Medieval Norwegian stave churches, some of which still stand today.

OPPOSITE: Students of a local vocational school were expertly guided through a plan that had many intricate details. They used beautiful materials and did a superb job.

6 A Walk in the Woods: Inspiring Treehouses Collected from All Over

Majestree, Out'n'About

Takilma, Oregon

It would only be fair to start this tour at Michael Garnier's "treesort," Out'n'About, in Takilma, Oregon.

Michael Garnier has taught me more about treehouses than anyone else. I met him in 1992, and he has been teaching me and countless others ever since. *Schooling* might be the more appropriate term in my case, as he has a quick wit and even quicker hands. I tend to be his foil during our annual World Treehouse Association conference gatherings, and Michael is a consummate showman. He is also whip smart, a superb dancer, and deadly serious about his treehouse craft.

Michael was an inspiration behind building our own bed-and-breakfast at Treehouse Point. He worked with Josephine County for eight years before they finally allowed his treesort to legally exist. I watched his struggles as he demonstrated the integrity of his structures, and treehouse builders will always be in his debt for the difficult trailblazing that he has done.

The latest addition to his eighteen-unit treesort is the Majestree (if you go to his website, www.treehouses.com, you will see that he plays with the word *tree* a lot). It is his highest residence and can fit up to six people comfortably. It has a full bathroom with toilet, sink, and shower, a queen-size bed in the main room, two double beds in the loft with an additional daybed, a compact kitchenette, and a porch with a spiral staircase to a private deck below. This magnificent abode is 47 feet up in a Douglas fir with some extraordinary custom woodwork inside and out.

PREVIOUS PAGE: A secondary tree, independent of the main structure, is used to bring people up from a lower deck to the treehouse above. Critical to its design is its flexibility. Note how the stair landing is able to slide as the trees move independently of each other.

OPPOSITE: The Majestree, at 47 feet above the ground, is an excellent example of a single-tree design that incorporates both beam-and-brace and cable support systems.

ABOVE LEFT: A bathroom so high in the trees is quite a luxury. Note the on-demand water heater above the toilet tank. Plumbing a treehouse is similiar to plumbing a regular house. Pipes flex with the tree.

ABOVE RIGHT: Michael Garnier demonstrates his style of the reverse triangle used to support heavy loads when there is an obstruction above and a less expensive suspender cannot be installed.

Santuario de Basurto

Woodinville, Washington

This stunning treehouse was born of a desire to build a children's tree fort. The project began with modest but lofty ideas. It soon expanded to encompass seven trees and new goals: The treehouse should be comfortable for adults as well as for kids, and materials should be sourced locally, repurposed whenever possible, and green. Thankfully, the Seattle area has many architectural salvage yards! Windows, doors, and flooring were all given second lives. Local western red cedar and Douglas fir were used whenever possible.

So the fort became a spectacular treehouse, which was built by David Gieson. The wraparound deck allows one to literally stroll about high in the forest. Views of the trees can be had from every angle. Indoors, the first-floor ceiling is high enough to make the room feel large and comfortable. Up the ship's ladder, the loft is the counterpoint to the main room: A low ceiling and foam bedding make for a very cozy, intimate atmosphere. Naps abound here. And atop all of this sits the cupola, from which one can see 360 degrees around the forest. Thoughtful lighting inside and out makes this treehouse a pleasure to be in and around.

Kids run laps around the deck and slide down the fire pole to the swings below. They run back up the stairs and climb to the cupola,

ABOVE: The multistory structure, complete with a wraparound deck, lights up a Pacific Northwest forest.

OPPOSITE: The treehouse stands tall in a mature Douglas fir forest. Its western red cedar railings are remnants from a huge treehouse job at Longwood Gardens in Pennsylvania.

OPPOSITE: Intricate trim work and thoughtful lighting create a warm and inviting wooden retreat.

TOP: Gieson's attention to detail is apparent in the interior finish work and exquisite furnishings.

ABOVE LEFT: Built-in shelving and windows cover every inch of this Arts and Crafts treehouse. It's particularly nice to see one of the support trees featured so prominently.

ABOVE RIGHT: A cozy sleeping loft leads by a ship's ladder to the lookout, which has a 360-degree view of the surrounding forest.

spying down on their friends. When the kids tire, the adults make their way to this treehouse, open a bottle of rum, and sit quietly talking on the back porch, their words mingling with the songs of birds. Santuario de Basurto translates as "Sanctuary in the Middle of the Forest."

Victor Brothers Treehouse

Western Washington

The first effort by the brothers Victor caught fire. The second—built in the same place—is indelibly printed in my mind as the most extraordinary and ambitious high school project ever realized. Most large-scale undertakings remain in the minds of cash-poor and unskilled teenagers. The brothers Victor, however, overcame the odds.

I have come to know these gentlemen well over the last several years. Michael, Paul, and Daniel are now in their twenties. Their father came to Treehouse Point to tell me of his sons' exploits, and when I arrived at their house—only ten minutes from my own—they had a Canon 5D camera trained on me the entire time. As it turned out, the brothers are deep into the digital world, and after I had them help me document our project at the WC Ranch, they decided it was time for a treehouse app for smartphones and tablets. I didn't know what that meant at the time, but I do now. True to form, they did another extraordinary job. It's called Treehouses of the Pacific Northwest. Please look it up!

OPPOSITE: Maple, Douglas fir, and hemlock trees support a wildly creative second effort by the three Victor brothers. The first treehouse that they built together at this location burned down.

BELOW: The hobbit door is surrounded by real rocks and masonry. It is holding up well despite its considerable weight and the inevitable movement from swaying trees.

OPPOSITE: The music room is reminiscent of the stern of an old sailing ship.

ABOVE: A full bar is a luxury all proper treehouses should afford. This one is put to good use, as I personally discovered during one of the brothers' renowned Christmas parties. Chain mail and a breastplate from a suit of armor allude to more fun that the brothers engage in at the treehouse.

BELOW: Avid gamers, the brothers have equipped the treehouse with five TVs—including one on the floor above this and another in the dungeon below—that are all networked so they can play against one another.

The HemLoft

Whistler, BC, Canada

Rookie builder Joel Allen went way out on a limb to build this marvelous masterpiece. With two architect buddies to help with design, and an acute shortage of both tools and materials, Joel crafted a most intricate and organic cocoon. Unfortunately, he built it on land that was not his own, and the cozy cob was doomed for removal. It will live on in many memories, as it took the Internet by storm and inspired many of us to reach for the highest branch and build our wildest dreams.

ABOVE: A thrilling walkway leads to the surreptitious cocoon tucked less than a mile off the nearest road in the backwoods of Whistler.

OPPOSITE: Looking through a skylight at the trunk of a mighty hemlock.

ABOVE: Gourmet camp meals are
prepared in the kitchen station.

BELOW: Lighting makes all the difference.
The curves of the walls make this
treehouse sublime.

ABOVE: Joel became a Craigslist expert and took full advantage of the deals that are plentiful on the website. He found more than $10,000 worth of free materials!

BELOW: Accents like the plant stand tell us much about the care and integrity of the man and his building acumen.

Rocky Mountain High

Evergreen, Colorado

Architect Missy Brown outdid herself on this idyllic design after attending a treehouse-building workshop with us in Washington State. Builders Bubba Smith and Daryl McDonald traveled to the foothills of the Rocky Mountains to bring to life her inspired vision. The treehouse serves as a relaxing space for Missy's brother and his family. To me, this sanctuary embodies all that a meticulously planned and beautifully crafted space can be. The feeling inside is one of tranquility and freedom—unbound from the demands of the earth below.

OPPOSITE: Flexibility is imperative in every treehouse design. Particularly when you are high off the ground in an exposed area. This treehouse has seen winds in excess of seventy miles an hour.

ABOVE: Weathered barn boards and corrugated metal are always in fashion with treehouse projects. A bridge or ramp is something I get a request for in almost every job.

TOP: Stained pine walls and salvaged fir roof rafters and sheathing lend warmth and authenticity. A small loft provides napping room for one.

ABOVE LEFT: The hog-wire railing fits well with the repurposed materials.

ABOVE RIGHT: A comfortable sitting nook provides an ideal place to unplug and relax.

OPPOSITE: A wall of books should be required in every treehouse. Here, architect Missy Brown even has a rolling library ladder to reach the highest volumes. The ladder also gives access to the loft that perches across the narrow space.

Dick and Charlie's Tea Room

Caddo Lake, near Uncertain, Texas

Lonnie Morrell owns and maintains a one-of-a-kind bayou-style treehouse that has as much history as it has love and dedication to keep it the way it is. On the shore of the mysterious Caddo Lake, a network of bayous spanning Texas and Louisiana, Dick and Charlie's Tea Room is said to be a relic of the years after Prohibition, when the citizens of Uncertain, Texas, in a dry county, would row across Big Cypress Bayou to patronize wet establishments in stilt houses and "beer boats" in the neighboring county. Lonnie's dad, J. R. "Dick" Morrell, bought the place for $1,000 in 1975, and Lonnie and his fishing buddies have kept the tea on ever since.

A sign posted outside captures the spirit of the place.

Dick and Charlie's Tea Room
House Rules:
1. There ain't any
2. There never was none
3. There ain't gonna be none

On a smaller sign below, it says:
Waitress wanted
Good fishing boat needed

LEFT: Cypress trees do 40 percent of the work of keeping Lonnie's treehouse from falling into the bayou; the rest is done by heavily compromised posts. Other nearby cypress trees, with their odd knees, may need to come to the rescue soon.

ABOVE: The sign that greets you is as much a warning as it is the law of the land.

Lonnie, who strives to keep the original feel of the place, has fastidiously preserved the period kitchen.

ABOVE: The treehouse tearoom hosts a merry band of Lonnie's oldest buddies, who I had the pleasure of spending the afternoon with at this one-of-a-kind retreat.

BELOW: A bedroom that appears to be dropping directly into the bayou is still used frequently, if only in the summer.

Attie Jonker's Treehouses

Lion's Lair

San Antonio, Texas

Attie Jonker once built safari camps in the Botswana bush country. They started as simple ground-based structures, but evolved into elaborate and often elevated wildlife observatories and retreats. Wise man that he is, Attie followed his American wife back to where she grew up, San Antonio, Texas, and picked up where he left off. He runs a creative building company, Green Wood Milling, and we are all lucky to have him in the States.

The oak hosting this curvaceous creation spreads 60 feet out in one direction in testament to the tree's incredible strength. A significant treehouse like this one doesn't even begin to register as a problem for a tree of this size.

OPPOSITE: The shingle work on this round pavilion speaks volumes about Attie's creative aesthetic. Attie sculpts functional art.

LEFT: Small details like iron rings and salvaged hardware accent his craft.

CENTER: The roof of the pavilion purposely opens to the lofty network of tree branches above. He frames its beauty with peeled mountain cedar rafters that are art pieces in their own right.

RIGHT: I cannot help wondering if the Texas-sized oak thinks that an enormous bird has nested in its branches.

The Lunch House

San Antonio, Texas

Ten-year-old Alex runs the show at the Lunch House. At least, that's what he thinks. Attie and I had a fun afternoon taking pictures at this treetop mini barn, and the young master made his apprehension over my appearance known. He simply wanted to use the tree fort, and I was in his way. On such a beautiful summer afternoon, I could hardly blame the little man.

LEFT: The trapdoor and playful ladder illustrate the level of detail Attie goes to in every project.

RIGHT: A barn door opens to a simple, three-season playhouse complete with a noisy winch used to raise and lower the lunch bucket.

OPPOSITE: Attie's ropework is just as refined as his woodwork, and a more enjoyable playhouse there could never be!

The Attic

San Antonio, Texas

Attie fashioned the siding for this Asian-influenced aerie out of the old fence that once surrounded this San Antonio home. It took two people two weeks to cut and apply the shingles, but it sets the place apart.

LEFT: No two of Attie's treehouses ever look the same. The steep roof and fish-scale siding make this a particularly playful building. It serves as a sophisticated family funhouse.

RIGHT: Details like custom screen windows and hand-carved window and door casings accent the equally intricate shingle pattern.

Cabin in the Trees

Ann Arbor, Michigan

Bruce Dondero promised his son Nick a treehouse when they discovered one of my books together nine years ago. After thinking, collecting, and dreaming—and countless hours of glorious work—Nick now believes anything his father tells him. It may have taken a few years, but all good things take time.

The only lumber purchased for the job was the framing for the platform. The cedar for the treehouse came from one of Bruce's customers (he's a housepainter) who was re-siding his house. Working together, father and son cleaned it up board by board. The redwood for the door and trim came from an old fence. The roof was inspired by a twenty-year-old article in *Mother Earth News*.

The bass is Bruce's. Nick, now fifteen, plays guitars and drums, and his brother plays keyboards.

ABOVE: Bruce admits to an affliction that many a carpenter suffers from—wood hoarding. It is just plain hard to throw good wood away. The redwood for the door and trim showed up last year as an old fence that had been replaced. Put it through the planer and WOW!

LEFT: Bruce and Nick's arboreal studio sits 11 feet off the ground on three spruce trees and a few spruce posts for good measure. It is 12 feet square and rises 12 feet to the peak. Everything but the platform is made from salvaged materials.

OPPOSITE: The siding came from a house that Bruce painted years ago. When the owners chose to re-side their home, Bruce asked if he could salvage the rough-sawn cedar. With a little love and care, he turned it into gold.

OVERLEAF: A simple open room is finished with materials collected over years. The vaulted roof distinguishes the treehouse as one of a kind. It is made from ten trusses, each built by layering three laminates of ¾-inch plywood. I can imagine the music sounding wonderful in a space like this.

The French Gardener's House

Annapolis, Maryland

I had the good fortune of meeting master landscaper Pierre Moitrier at a building workshop in Virginia a few years back. After we taught him everything we know about building treehouses, he shared with us some photos of the treehouse that he had just completed in his backyard in Annapolis. It turned out he already knew everything that he needed to know. And I ended up learning more from him—like how to decorate in a sophisticated French style. *Mais oui*!

OPPOSITE: A maple in Pierre's backyard gave the landscape architect the idea to rise above his manicured yard for a better view.

ABOVE: A trapdoor with antique hardware is counterbalanced by a weight, making entry easier when coming up from below.

RIGHT: Fabrics adorn the walls and ceiling of the simple abode, lending softness and warmth to the rustic shelter.

OVERLEAF: A crystal chandelier highlights the simple decor.

Roderick Romero's Treehouses

All of these treehouses were designed and built by Roderick Romero. I greatly admire Roderick's commitment to his vision. The sculptural qualities of his tree structures captivate, the heights are often dizzying (and they are strictly tree-supported), and he always sources interesting and hard-to-find recycled materials. The results are everything treehouses should be.

Dogwood Farm

Connecticut

A private client was looking for a sculptural outlook from which to view a vast and undulating property. Roderick is never afraid of placing his creations high in appropriate trees and he is always careful to use interesting recycled materials so that the exposed structure does not look like it came straight out of a local "big box" lumber store.

LEFT: The chosen materials blend well with three stellar support oaks and the forest behind.

RIGHT: Protecting a stair entrance with additional railing is critical at such high elevations. It is also nice to have a landing somewhere along the way. This gives the designer a chance to change the staircase's direction and alert the visitor that their outlook is about to change.

OPPOSITE: The Dogwood Farm treehouse soars 24 feet above the ground and lifts the spirits of all who have the privilege to visit. The beam layout in this three-tree scenario is a little tricky, however. It is imperative that the trees be allowed to move independently of each other, and the distances they move relative to one another can be huge—especially at higher elevations.

Lake Spectacle

Connecticut

Every time I visit one of Roderick's "babies," I smile. In this case I nearly cried tears of joy! His signature weaving of branches in bird's nest intricacy greets you and pulls you in on a journey to a carefree world of lake views and lemonade.

OPPOSITE ABOVE: A large white oak anchors the entry stair and bridge that lead 30 feet to a world apart. A lake view awaits at the main platform, along with an octagonal clubhouse that can serve a thousand purposes.

OPPOSITE BELOW LEFT: Bridges of this scale pull on the trees with tremendous force. The anchors are short-armed TABs (6-inch boss and 4-inch arm, typically) that are sunk well into the wood of a healthy tree. Heavy chains with a turnbuckle at one end stretch between TABs on both sides of the walkway. Galvanized carriage bolts secure bridge decking through openings in the chain links. Standard manila rope railing is a bad idea. This is

a synthetic manila called Hempex that will not shrink or stretch in varying weather conditions.

OPPOSITE BELOW RIGHT: Stairs wind up the trunk without making excessive penetrations into the tree. The stair stringers land on occasional beam-and-brace struts that are visible in the photograph above this one. A sturdy Roman cross–style platform awaits at the top of the stairs and also supports one side of the bridge.

ABOVE: The simple interior of the octagonal aerie is a collection of interesting "mushroom wood" walls, salvaged pine floors, and an eclectic array of antique doors and windows.

OPPOSITE: Cedars support an otherworldly Romero creation. Uniform railings front an organic collection of round windows fashioned from heavily textured mushroom wood—a material favored by the designer. It comes from mushroom farms in the Northeast, where it is used for growing platforms. Acid in compost distresses its surface. Growers sell the wood in the recycled lumber market.

ABOVE LEFT: Barn doors open wide to welcome visitors from an ample deck into a space like the hull of a cabin cruiser.

ABOVE RIGHT: Sarah Jefferson, a net builder, came from Washington State to ply her trade of crafting used fishing nets into huge hammocks that stretch between trees.

BELOW RIGHT: Small spaces appear larger when they open up to the front. It's a nice trick that often comes in handy when building in the trees.

JEM Treehouse

Southampton, New York

The name of this treehouse comes from the initials of the client's children. Where the design comes from, only Roderick knows. I think it is remarkable. What is also remarkable is the skill of the carpenters who executed the plan and the wonderful materials they employed.

Lake Nest Treehouse

Southampton, New York

As it sometimes happens with treehouse projects, forgiveness from building authorities must be asked for after the fact. In this case, Roderick engaged the services of a local architect and a bargain was struck to allow this two-tiered functional sculpture to remain. It would have been a shame to see such a lovely aerie succumb to the nonsense of an inflexible bureaucracy. Instead it stands as an example of how magic can happen when people simply talk with one another to find common ground and, in this case, common air.

ABOVE: The huge tree sprouts through the upper deck and shields the adventurous under its leafy canopy on hot summer days.

BELOW: A beguiling stairway of branch work and salvaged Southern yellow pine lure upward all who wander close.

OPPOSITE: When I see something like this, I wonder if humans are meant to be in trees again. Or if, in fact, trees themselves are beckoning to us to return and reside among their boughs.

Old N.W. Road House

East Hampton, New York

My grandparents lived on Long Island, and my parents had friends we would visit farther out. Every time I return to Long Island's East End I think of summer, and a treehouse like this is what summer is all about.

OPPOSITE: Wide eaves help shade the treehouse from the summer sun.

ABOVE LEFT: The simplest structures are often the most beautiful.

ABOVE RIGHT: There is something appealing about having a tree come right through your living room. Just know that there regularly will be maintenance issues with the roof if you need the house to remain waterproof.

BELOW: Early treehouse design options from Roderick are framed on the back wall. A translucent art piece forms a window in the center.

James "B'fer" Roth's Treehouses

Michael's Memorial

Warren, Vermont

James "B'fer" Roth builds beautiful, heartfelt treehouses and rustic furniture in Vermont's heartland. Formerly the lead designer and builder of a company that specialized in wheelchair-accessible treehouses, he now runs a company called, simply, The Treehouse Guys.

One afternoon, B'fer received a call from an acquaintance asking if he might help create a long-dreamed-about treehouse in the man's backyard. The kicker was that the man, Michael, had been recently diagnosed with pancreatic cancer and had only a few short months to live.

The result is a structure built with playful integrity and pure love.

BELOW: A dead hemlock in Michael's backyard was the impetus for renewal and rebirth. In the old tree's place, a new point of interest, an inspiration, stands as a memorial to an artistic soul who left this earth far too soon.

RIGHT: Playful use of recycled doors, windows, and bicycle wheels give insight into who the wonderful man, Michael, was.

BELOW RIGHT: Locust log posts do the work that the once-proud hemlock can no longer do. Branch-and-wire bracing will ensure stability for many years to come. It is said that locust posts can be planted directly in the ground and last for fifty years.

Zeno Mountain Farm

Lincoln, Vermont

OPPOSITE ABOVE: Two treehouse cabins sleep the campers. This one, called A Long Way Up, hangs from beech and maple trees and locust log posts. The main cabin sleeps twelve and the structure on the right houses the bath facilities.

I was fortunate to build with B'fer a few years back in Pennsylvania, and I am pleased to see his beautiful work continue. Here, his craft goes on at Zeno Mountain Farm in Lincoln, Vermont. The farm is an organization that runs camps for people with and without disabilities. They have a great website, so please check it out at www.zenomountainfarm.org!

LEFT: Grandpa's Treehouse, named for its sponsor, sleeps eighteen campers and on nicer days looks out over a vast Vermont vista. Plumbing a treehouse is a question people often ask about. The white plastic pipe in this photograph indicates that plumbing for waste is not much different from plumbing a regular house—but here you have a much larger "crawlspace" to work in!

ABOVE: Quirky windows define B'fer's treehouse designs, as do the rustic materials that he sources from local mom-and-pop sawmills.

ABOVE: Only experienced campers are allowed the top bunks in this network of nighttime nests. West-facing windows let the summertime sleepers get as much shut-eye as the camp counselors allow.

OPPOSITE: The forest appears to come inside where a rookery of sleeping nests fills the canopy.

Topridge

Upstate New York

A few years ago, our company had a treehouse story appear in
Architectural Digest. It caught the eye of a whimsical property owner
in New York and was passed to the property manager and then into
the hands of a carpenter named Jim. That was the beginning of what
turned into a most extraordinary and ambitious arboreal undertaking.
Good planning and attention to detail assured success, and I am proud
to add that Jim, charged with building the one-off perch, attended one
of our building workshops in Washington State. Little did we know at
the time what Jim was capable of.

Used as a guesthouse, it sleeps four adults comfortably and
boasts a full bathroom with hot and cold running water. Outside, a
meandering stairway threads up through mature hemlocks to a height
that can exceed 25 feet above the forest floor. Outdoor decks and
walkways surround the entire structure and provide outlooks to the
forest and adjacent lake.

The lofty retreat was carefully engineered. An effort of this
magnitude absolutely requires the attention and blessing of a
professional structural engineer. For this project Charley Greenwood
of Greenwood Engineering in Oregon stepped up in brilliant fashion. I
can imagine he was a source of consternation for Jim and the building
team, as complex building jobs will often outstretch the patience of
many a carpenter, but the design was followed faithfully, and despite
a midwinter build in the wild North Country, Jim orchestrated a
flawless execution of the plan.

After seven seasons aloft, the building is wearing well. At such
heights, the worry is that the trees will move radically in high winds
and damage themselves, the structure, or both. In fact, after the 2011
hurricane that wreaked havoc throughout New England and upstate
New York, the treehouse came through with flying colors—a tribute to
all involved: the owner, the engineer, the builders, and especially the
trees themselves.

LEFT: The Adirondack camp building style
is alive and well in its native land. Here
the bark-on-branch work leads to a
heavenly treetop haven.

RIGHT: The substructure is nearly as
beautiful to observe as the structure
above. The center post is a hollowed-out
log that houses all of the treehouses'
utility lines.

OPPOSITE: Carpenter Jim, the man behind
the saw on this wondrous masterpiece,
participated in one of our treehouse-
building workshops in 2006. Little did we
know at the time what he was capable
of, though I had my suspicions.

ABOVE: The treehouse serves as sleeping quarters for a lucky few who visit the summer camp. This is the master suite that greets you directly from the entry door.

LEFT: The entry door is a work of art in itself. Walnut panels below the inlaid tree branches open to screens that allow cross ventilation, but not bugs and buzzing insects.

OPPOSITE ABOVE: A satellite bedroom sleeps two more.

OPPOSITE BELOW: A burl sink took countless hours to finish and sets the tone for the lavish full bathroom.

Drynachan Lodge Treehouse

Cawdor, Scotland

WSJ., the *Wall Street Journal*'s magazine, was laying out at my sister-in-law's house when she remembered to show me an article about a young family that was transforming their ancient Scottish family estate into a partridge-shooting lodge. And they had a treehouse. Only weeks later Judy and I found ourselves hurtling through the desolate Scottish moor in a rental car, searching out the Drynachan Valley and the current thane of Cawdor and builder of said structure.

Lord Cawdor, or Colin, as he prefers to be called, moved his new wife, Isabella, to this 80-square-mile family estate in 1994 with the intention of sprucing up land that had been in the family for 800 years and being closer to the place where he would raise a family. Trained as an architect at the Pratt Institute in New York City, he instead wandered into finance and found himself commuting between London and "the farm" on weekends. Meanwhile, his four children were growing up in an idyllic setting. As a way of connecting with them, he built his masterwork in ancient alders on the banks of the River Findhorn between 2003 and 2005. It was built for the kids, but it was really a therapy project for Colin to get away from thoughts of work back in London.

Year one produced a platform squarely nailed to the trunks of the alders with two-by-sixes, and little room for growth or movement. Year two yielded the house itself, cobbled from old doors and windows that he found stashed in buildings around the estate. The steep roof and requisite dormer proved more than he could build himself, so he hired a local roofer for that.

OPPOSITE: Lord Cawdor, a trained architect, assembled doors and windows that were stashed in outbuildings on his Scottish family estate. He turned them into this riverside retreat high on the trunks of several old and weathered alder trees.

ABOVE: A glimpse between the trees from the riverbank below reveals a different view of the newest building on the 80-square-mile family estate.

BELOW: Prayer flags shudder in the wind and welcome visitors to a peaceful sanctuary on the River Findhorn.

At first the kids were intimidated by all the glass, but now his sixteen-year-old is spending more time in the treehouse—especially when she has friends visiting.

Treehouse building, in a sense, goes a very long way back in the Cawdor family. The original castle, where Colin's stepmother still lives, was built around an enormous holly tree—quite literally. The tree was encased in the grand stair foyer where, without all of the tree's needs met, it died, but it remains to this day. Colin's father had the tree carbon-dated to get a better idea of when the castle was actually built. The results showed somewhere around 1340 or 1350. While his ancestors built a tree into a house, Colin built a house in a tree.

ABOVE: Salvaged windows, thoughtfully arranged, make up the entire west end of the small space.

TOP RIGHT: There is room above for Colin and Isabella's four children to share sleepover rights.

CENTER: A seagrass rug and an eclectic collection of simple furnishings are all that adorn a cheery, light-filled room.

BELOW: A farm table awaits the next heated board game or family picnic. Outside, the River Findhorn quietly rolls by.

Tyrolean Treetop

Mariastein, Austria

Bernd Weinmayer is a glass artist of the highest order. His creations are on display in a glassblowing studio that he built twenty years ago on his family's property at the foot of the awe-inspiring Austrian Alps.

It turns out that Bernd is a crafty woodworker as well.

A few years ago he sent some photos of a treehouse that he decided to build on the edge of a forest directly behind his shop. Perched atop a living tree that had lost its crown in a storm, it was a place to climb up to, unplug, and recharge his creative soul.

When I contacted him, I was distressed to hear that a beetle infestation had killed his tree.

Rather than abandon ship, Bernd chose to rescue the abode by cutting it down. He called a crane buddy to balance and keep everything upright, and proceeded to relocate the entire structure to an outside corner of his studio.

Having now witnessed firsthand Bernd's building acumen, it was no surprise to see the beefiness of the concrete retaining walls that held the earth back from his semisubterranean glass studio. Relocating the treehouse simply involved designing and fabricating a footing that he could bolt to the concrete walls to support his previously ill-fated aerie.

He did a wonderful job

OPPOSITE: The Tyrolean Alps rise high in the background of this towering hermitage. This is the retreat of a famous glassblower, whose studio is built into a hillside just below.

LEFT: Wood-boring beetles attacked the tree in its former location, so Bernd decided to cut and move the fracas, treehouse and all, to a sturdy location steps outside of his office.

CENTER: Bernd fits a lot into a tight space, as all good treehouses should. Be careful with woodstoves, however. They can generate more heat than a small space can comfortably handle.

RIGHT: Tyrolean cowbells alert us to the arrival of visitors below.

Art Farm

Kalamata, Greece

Sotiris Marinis is a man of indeterminate age. He looks like he could be in his forties, but his bright, burning eyes, wild gray hair, and knowing smile reveal the wisdom of a man much older. Olive trees and the oils they yield play a role in keeping him young, and now olive tree huts, or *eleokalyves*, are taking center stage in his play with age.

This is not the first time that treehouses have played a role in Sotiris's life. At eleven years old, he became famous in his village for building a treehouse with lights. Each summer he would build a small hut in the moria trees near the beach. There was no electricity in his town, and at an expo in Athens he learned to use a simple battery, switch, wire, and a lightbulb. People were amazed. These were the first lights in the area. His mother said, "My brilliant son! You should become an electrician!" Which he did.

Sotiris had a long career as an electrical engineer. Now he is the owner of a five-acre "art camp" that houses guests in rustic olive tree huts that overlook the turquoise Aegean Sea.

His style of building treehouses is all his own.

Wood platforms, some fashioned from large wooden wire wheels, balance low in the olive's branches—sometimes posted to the ground with 2-inch round steel columns. From there he creates a light steel rebar framework that he welds together himself. The frame serves as the house's shell and a surface on which to attach the different layers of construction—first a layer of light bamboo to lend the interior warmth, then a layer of plastic to keep out the elements. Finally, he goes down to the river and harvests reeds to finish the outside and weave the doors and windows. It is simple, and in the climate of southern Greece, it works.

The Art Farm is a dream in the making. A 750-person amphitheater is nearing completion, and a building to house an artisan blacksmith, cheese maker, and, of course, olive oil producer is awaiting funding. Judging by the progress he has made in four short years, there is no doubt that the art camp hotel will be a beautiful success.

ABOVE: Olive trees were not high on my list of suitable treehouse trees until I visited Sotiris Marinis's farm in the famous Kalamata olive region of Greece.

OPPOSITE: Sotiris used a large wooden wire spool for the floor of his simple tree hut. He harvested reeds from a local river for use as siding and roofing.

OPPOSITE: I had the company of two white cats that followed me from hut to hut as I took my pictures. Despite not advertising, the cats are not the only visitors to the Art Farm. Backpackers routinely hear of the place through the grapevine and arrive unannounced.

ABOVE LEFT: Tea is set for two in the smallest of the tree huts. The floor area is only seven feet in diameter.

ABOVE RIGHT: The largest of the four tree huts is supported by two posts and an olive tree. It is only 5 feet wide and 10 feet long.

BELOW LEFT: There is something highly romantic about sleeping in a tree. Doing so in Greece only adds to the appeal.

BELOW RIGHT: Bathroom facilities and a communal kitchen are only a few steps away from all of the elevated reed houses. They serve simply as places to sleep, relax, and seek shelter from the hot sun.

Dylan's Africa

In November of 2012, Dylan Rauch, a key member of my carpentry team and new photographer, set out on a journey to Zimbabwe to visit his mother, a Fulbright scholar, in the capital city of Harare. With so much happening on the treehouse front at home, we determined that this would be the perfect opportunity to see what kinds of tree structures sub-Saharan Africa had to offer. Dylan extended his trip by a few weeks for an epic adventure in treehouse scouting, traveling everywhere from the deltas of Botswana to a remote island off the coast of Kenya. His steady demeanor and adventurous spirit made him the perfect man for the job and led him to discover some truly incredible treehouses. It was a tough job, but someone had to do it.

Tongabezi Lodge Treehouse

Livingstone, Zambia

After spending a couple of weeks exploring Zimbabwe with his mother, Carol, and teaching carpentry at Chiedza Child Care Center, Dylan set off on his treehouse adventure. First stop: Livingstone, Zambia. After a roundabout airplane journey via Johannesburg, South Africa, Dylan landed in Zambia, where he was greeted by a man named Faden, who drove him to the Tongabezi Lodge, a lavish resort built along the bank of the Zambezi River. Dylan found himself in the setting of a truly luxurious, romantic getaway in a wild place— complete with vervet monkeys swinging around and the snorts of hippos in the not-so-far distance. The grounds run along the contour of the riverbank, and a narrow walkway that winds along leads guests to the private love nest that rests in the boughs of the trees. The open-air treehouse is perched right over the river and nestled up against a textured cliff face that makes up the only full wall in the structure. The treehouse is fully equipped with a claw-foot tub and toilet, and it overlooks the river that marks the border between Zambia and Zimbabwe. A luxurious king-size bed and sitting area make this treehouse top-notch—according to our lucky traveler.

This open-air guesthouse sits on the bank of the Zambezi river. Guests can soak up the beauty of their surroundings while they relax on a pine deck.

ABOVE: This exotic treehouse is fully equipped with a private shower and a claw-foot tub.

BELOW: The bathroom mirror reflects the stunning view.

RIGHT: The structure's rear wall is basalt rock, and trunks of a riverine ebony tree rise through the floor.

OPPOSITE: Sitting in an old-growth jackalberry tree, this treehouse is built from local materials. The lower level is a bathroom that has hot and cold solar-powered running water.

ABOVE: The elevated lodge looks out over the surrounding bush and floodplains that host an incredible array of wildlife, including giraffes, leopards, and elephants.

BELOW: A small set of steps leads down to the cocktail deck from the sleeping area.

Delta Camp Treehouse

Botswana

After being pampered in Zambia, Dylan flew on to Maun, Botswana, by way of Johannesburg. It was there that he was met by a private plane piloted by a woman named Tepo-Tepo (which translates to "trust"), who flew him over the vast Okavango Delta, the largest inland delta in the world, and safely landed their Cessna on a small dirt runway amid the lush waterways. Three luxury safari camps are tucked neatly into the delta, which is navigated by canoe. The water level happened to be low when Dylan visited, and when night fell, the glow of wildfires burning in the distance created a spectacular sight. After a minor detour due to an elephant crossing, Dylan was led to Delta Camp Treehouse by his three hosts, Poison (so dubbed for his deadly skills on the soccer field), Matt, and Ponay, the manager. The treehouse is built in two jackalberry trees, the Latin name of which is *Diospyros mespiliformis*, a fact that Poison, the resident naturalist, recited from memory. The structure has two stories connected by a staircase that leads first to the facilities—complete with a toilet, sink, and shower. Continuing up the staircase, you arrive at the second story, which includes a charming bedroom and a cocktail deck that is perched over a lagoon. The billowy white mosquito net curtains give the treehouse an airy and romantic feel—making this another love nest suspended within the African wilderness.

BELOW: Salvaged wood makes up the floorboards, and hand-carved shelving demonstrates the skills of the local craftsmen.

OPPOSITE ABOVE: A cocktail deck overlooks a favorite watering hole for local wildlife.

OPPOSITE BELOW: A queen-size bed is perched on the upper floor of this classic treehouse. Equipped with mosquito netting, the bed has 360-degree views of the savanna.

Tarangire Treetops

Tanzania

OPPOSITE: Here is one of the twenty elevated tree rooms at Tarangire Treetops. The screened-in porch creates an open-air feel and presents an expansive view of the Tarangire plains.

BELOW: Locally made furnishings, an exposed baobab branch, and a king-size bed fill the luxurious guest room.

OVERLEAF: This baobab tree is estimated to be one thousand years old and has a hollow center filled with water, allowing it to survive during severe droughts.

On the third leg of his journey, Dylan found himself flying above Kilimanjaro and into an airport outside of Arucha, Tanzania. After a three-hour car ride through the arid desert of Kenya and into the rocky terrain of northeast Tanzania, Dylan arrived at the Tarangire Treetops resort. Massive baobab trees measuring about 12–16 feet in diameter greeted Dylan as he explored another deluxe establishment. Baobab trees have an incredible water-retention system in which water is stored in the hollow middle of these broad trees. Treehouses are not the only abodes situated within the baobab trees; bats often make their homes in rotted-out cavities of these gentle giants. The property has twenty luxurious elevated houses making up the safari resort. The screened-in houses allow guests to enjoy the fresh air and wildlife from the comfort of the treetops.

One Love Island Treehouse

Ngomeni, Kenya

After hearing about a small treehouse on remote One Love Island off the coast of Kenya, Dylan embarked on the last leg of his journey. A plane ride, a *matato* (minibus), a "drive-yourself taxi," and a kind man named Madi led him to a little village called Ngomeni. It was there that Dylan was met by Captain Ali, who silently canoed him, guided by the light of the full moon, across the turquoise Ungwana Bay to the island. White sand and tropical palm trees surround the island, which serves as a hostel and public lounge space for the people of nearby villages. The charming treehouse is built using wood from mangrove trees and reeds from the local area. Despite there being no amenities on the island, Dylan was fed delicious lobster dinners and slept in an open-air pavilion during the intensely hot and humid afternoon.

I can't promise that everyone who comes to work for Nelson Treehouse and Supply will have these kinds of experiences and opportunities, but it will always be something that we keep our eyes and ears open for! Well done, Dylan. And thank you.

ABOVE: A view of the Indian Ocean. The picturesque One Love Island is used as a hostel and public park for the people of Ngomeni.

OPPOSITE: The charming structure is used for overnight accommodations and as an escape from the sweltering sun.

Sources

TREEHOUSE DESIGN, CONSTRUCTION, AND SUPPLY

TABs and other treehouse hardware described in this book can be purchased from the companies listed as carrying treehouse hardware below. The instructions in the book are tailored to the hardware sold by Nelson Treehouse and Supply. Specifications for hardware from other suppliers may vary, but the general function is the same and guidelines for installation are similar.

Azzanarts (Attie Jonker), San Antonio, Texas
Treehouse design and construction
www.azzanarts.com

Barbara Butler, San Francisco, California
Treehouse design and construction
www.barbarabutler.com

Barefoot Builders (Michael Murphy), Tacoma, Washington
Treehouse design and construction
www.barefoottreehouses.com

Greenwood Engineering (Charles Greenwood), Cave Junction, Oregon
Treehouse engineer, treehouse hardware
www.treehouseengineering.com

Hampus, Hillerod, Denmark
Treehouse design and construction
www.hampus.dk

La Cabane Perchée (Alain Laurens), Saint Saturnin d'Apt, France
Treehouse design and construction
http://www.la-cabane-perchee.com/

Living Tree Online (Jonathan Fairoaks), Glenmoore, Pennsylvania
Treehouse design and construction, consulting arborist
www.thelivingtreehouse.com

Michael Ince, Brookhaven, New York
Sculptor and treehouse artist
(631) 286-5870

Nelson Treehouse and Supply (Pete Nelson), Fall City, Washington
Treehouse design and construction, treehouse hardware
www.nelsontreehouseandsupply.com

Out'n'About (Michael Garnier), Takilma, Oregon
Treehouse design and construction, treehouse hardware
www.treehouses.com

Romero Studios (Roderick Romero), New York, New York
Treehouse design and construction
www.romerostudios.com

Treehouse Creations (Kobayashi Takashi), Tokyo, Japan
Treehouse design and construction
www.treehouse.jp

The Treehouse Guys (James "B'fer" Roth and Chris "Ka-V" Haake), Warren, Vermont
Treehouse design and construction
www.treehouses.org

Tree Top Builders (Dan Wright), West Chester, Pennsylvania
Treehouse design and construction, treehouse hardware
www.treetopbuilders.net

Wild Tree Woodworks (David Geisen), Seattle, Washington
Treehouse design and construction
www.wildtreewoodworks.com

ARBORISTS AND OTHER USEFUL EXPERTS

BT Big Timberworks, Gallatin Gateway, Montana
Extraordinary builders
www.bigtimberworks.com

Dan Mack, Warwick, New York
Furniture builder and wood sculptor
www.danielmack.com

Designs for Greener Gardens (Pierre Moitrier), Annapolis, Maryland
Landscape design, consulting arborist
www.greenergardens.net

Fire Tower Engineered Timber (Ben Brungraber), Providence, Rhode Island
Engineer
www.ftet.biz

Hugh Lofting Timber Framing (Hugh Lofting), West Grove, Pennsylvania
Timber framing
www.hughloftingtimberframe.com

Out on a Limb Tree Company (Kathy Holzer), Seattle, Washington
Arborist/tree service and women's world tree-climbing champion
www.outonalimbseattle.com

Ribeiro Tree Consultants (Dr. Olaf K. Ribeiro), Bainbridge Island, Washington
Plant Pathologist
ribeirotreeconsultants.com

Salisbury Woodworking (Tim Salisbury), Bainbridge Island, Washington
Wood floors and timber framing
www.salisburywoodworking.com

Studio Cortés (Carlos Cortés), San Antonio, Texas
Faux Bois specialty work
www.studiocortes.com

Tree Solutions (Scott D. Baker), Seattle, Washington
Consulting arborist
www.treesolutions.net

Treehouse ARTZ (Jake Jacob), Port Townsend, Washington
Arborwork, rigging, timbers, ziplines
www.treehouseartz.com

Treehouse Workshop (Pete Nelson & Jake Jacob), Fall City, Washington
Treehouse building workshops for aspiring treehouse builders
www.treehouseworkshop.com

Urban Forest Innovations (Philip van Wassenaer), Mississauga, Canada
Consulting arborist
www.urbanforestinnovations.com

SUPPLIES OF ALL KINDS

American Arborist Supplies, West Chester, Pennsylvania
Rigging, climbing, safety gear, and tree care
www.arborist.com

Brion Toss Yacht Riggers (Brion Toss), Port Townsend, Washington
Rigging of all kinds
www.briontoss.com

Cape Cleare Fishery (Rick Oltman), Port Townsend, Washington
Premium quality wild Alaskan salmon, sustainably harvested direct from the fishermen
www.capecleare.com

ConvectAir, Sainte-Thérèse, Canada
Electric home heating solutions
www.convectair.com

Crenshaw Lighting (Woody Crenshaw),
Floyd, Virginia
Lighting
www.crenshawlighting.com

Diamond Pier, Gig Harbor, Washington
Building foundation systems
www.diamondpier.com

Duluth Timber Company, Duluth,
Minnesota
Reclaimed wood
www.duluthtimber.com

Earthwise Architectural Salvage, Seattle,
Washington
Reclaimed building materials
www.earthwise-salvage.com

Green Wood Milling Company (Attie
Jonker), San Antonio, Texas
Reclaimed wood
www.greenwoodmilling.com

Incinolet, Dallas, Texas
Electric incinerating toilet
www.incinolet.com

Lindal Cedar Homes, Seattle,
Washington
Great Douglas fir wood windows
www.lindal.com

New Tribe, Grants Pass, Oregon
Tree climbing equipment
www.newtribe.com

Pioneer Millworks, Farmington, New
York
Reclaimed wood
www.pioneermillworks.com

Screw Products, Gig Harbor, Washington
Star drive wood screws—the ultimate
www.screw-products.com

Second Use, Seattle, Washington
Reclaimed building materials
www.seconduse.com

TerraMai, White City, Oregon
Reclaimed wood
www.terramai.com

WesSpur Tree Equipment, Bellingham,
Washington
Rigging, climbing, and safety gear
www.wesspur.com

ORGANIZATIONS, USEFUL AND INSPIRATIONAL

Building Materials Reuse Association
(BMRA)
www.bmra.org

The Hole in the Wall Gang Camp
No-fee camp for youth, ages seven to
fifteen, with cancer and serious blood
diseases
www.holeinthewallgang.org

International Society of Arborculture
www.isa-arbor.com

IslandWood, Bainbridge Island,
Washington
Environmental learning center
www.islandwood.org

Julia Butterfly Hill
www.juliabutterfly.com

Longwood Gardens, Kennett Square,
Pennsylvania
www.longwoodgardens.org

Make a Wish Foundation
www.wish.org

U.S. Green Building Council
www.usgbc.org

TREEHOUSE LODGING AROUND THE WORLD

Ariaú Amazon Towers, Manaus, Brazil
www.ariautowers.com

Baumhaushotel, Neisseaue, Germany
Located at builder/genius Jurgen
Bergmann's amusement park,
Kulturinsel Einsiedel
www.kulturinsel.de

Cedar Creek Treehouse, Ashford,
Washington
www.cedarcreektreehouse.com

Davis Ranch Retreat, Bastrop, Texas
www.davisranchretreat.com

Finca Bellavista, La Florida De Osa,
Costa Rica
Matt and Erica Hogan's treehouse
community and resort
www.fincabellavista.net

Free Spirit Spheres, Qualicum Beach,
Canada
Treehouse visionary Tom Chudleigh's
creation
www.freespiritspheres.com

Green Magic Resort, Wayanad, India
www.greenmagicresort.com

Hotell Hackspett, Västerås, Sweden
www.mikaelgenberg.com

Khao Sok Tree House Resort, Tar,
Thailand
www.khaosok-treehouse.com

Oddballs' Palm Island Luxury Lodge,
Maun, Botswana
www.oddballscamp.com

Out'n'About, Takilma, Oregon
Treehouse pioneer Michael Garnier's
"treesort"
www.treehouses.com

Pia Treehouse, Pai, Maehongson,
Thailand
www.paitreehouse.com

Safari Land, Bokkapuram, Masinagudi,
India
www.safarilandresorts.com

Sanya Nanshan Treehouse Resort and
Beach Club, Hainan, China
www.treehousesofhawaii.com

Tarangire Treetops, Tarangire, Tanzania
www.elewanacollection.com

Tongabezi Lodge, Livingston, Zambia
www.tongabezi.com

Treehouse Point, Issaquah, Washington
Pete and Judy Nelson's treehouse B&B
www.treehousepoint.com

As always, please send photos of
and information about your most
inspirational treehouse projects to
info@nelsontreehouseandsupply.com.

Index

Photo Credits

Acknowledgments

First and foremost I thank
Daryl McDonald, our foreman,
and builder in the most honorable
sense of the word. I would not
have had much to show over the
last fifteen years without him.

And the crew that builds with him:
Joel "Bubba" Smith
Chuck McClellen
Charlie Nelson
Henry Nelson
Dylan Rauch
Rheanna Pless
Toby Malloy
Alex Meyer
Ian Franks
Devin Hanley
Buffie Parks
Patrick Willse

**Our other building friends
and family:**
Jake Jacob
Seanix Zenobia
Ian Weedman
Josh Barnes
Steve Wray
Bruce Blacker
Tom Keugler
Charley Greenwood
John Cage
Sarah J
Cave
Raphael Serna
Bartosz Sikorski

Inspirators and Helpers:
Judy Nelson
Emily Nelson
Andrew Evans
Andrea Scott
Claudia Christen

Christopher Richter
Dave Fall
Daniel Ash
Kelly Rush
John Shulthers
Madeline Goryl
Eric Teitelbaum
Sue Holbink
Ed Hazen
Roderick Romero
Michael Garnier
Nancy Coffin DeFeyter
Don DeFeyter
Michael Victor
Paul Victor
Gail Reed from Safari Experts
Russell Coxen
Dave Duce
Mark Grove
Troy Queen
Tory Jones
Larry Brown
Harry Barnes
Kathy Lambert
Dave Egan
Peter Jewett
Jason Carey
Ben Dey

At Abrams:
Eric Himmel
Darilyn Carnes
Anet Sirna-Bruder
Lauren Hougen
Jacqueline Bondanza
Susan Homer

To Norman, my father,
who led an exemplary life.
He opened my eyes
to all the things I love.

—Pete Nelson

Designer: Darilyn Lowe Carnes
Production Manager: Anet Sirna-Bruder

Library of Congress Control Number: 2013945694

ISBN: 978-1-4197-1171-8

Printed and bound in the United States
10 9 8 7 6 5 4 3 2 1

Abrams books are available at special discounts when
purchased in quantity for premiums and promotions as
well as fundraising or educational use. Special editions
can also be created to specification. For details, contact
specialsales@abramsbooks.com or the address below.

THE ART OF BOOKS SINCE 1949

115 West 18th Street
New York, NY 10011
www.abramsbooks.com

NE   4/2014